Journey to Literacy:
No Worksheets Required

Krista Flemington
Linda Hewins
Una Villiers

Pembroke Publishers Limited

To young children and their hard-working teachers who provide engaging literacy experiences

© **2011 Pembroke Publishers**
538 Hood Road
Markham, Ontario, Canada L3R 3K9
www.pembrokepublishers.com

Distributed in the U.S. by Stenhouse Publishers
480 Congress Street
Portland, ME 04101
www.stenhouse.com

We acknowledge the financial support of the Government of Canada through the Book Publishing Industry Development Program (BPIDP) for our publishing activities.

We acknowledge the assistance of the Government of Ontario through the Ontario Media Development Corporation's Ontario Book Initiative.

Library and Archives Canada Cataloguing in Publication

Flemington, Krista
    Journey to literacy : no worksheets required : kindergarten literacy centres that motivate young learners to succeed / Krista Flemington, Linda Hewins, Una Villiers.

Includes bibliographical references and index.
Issued also in electronic formats.
ISBN 978-1-55138-261-6

    1. Language arts (Kindergarten). 2. Literacy — Study and teaching (Preschool).
3. Kindergarten — Activity programs. I. Hart-Hewins, Linda II. Villiers, Una III. Title.

LB1181.F64 2011   372.6'049   C2011-900755-X

Editor: Kate Revington
Cover Design: John Zehethofer
Typesetting: JayTee Graphics

Printed and bound in Canada
9 8 7 6 5 4 3 2 1

Contents

Introduction: Beyond Worksheets to Learning Centres

Today's Kindergarten classrooms welcome children that are part of a rapidly changing world, accompanied by exploding technology. Teachers must meet that challenge and provide all children with an inviting environment which honors their individual differences, respects their developmental levels, and stimulates them to learn.

Certain trends in teaching run counter to meeting this challenge. In light of the current emphasis on early literacy development — as well as the pressure of extensive curriculum expectations — many Kindergarten teachers have resorted to using worksheets and issuing teacher-directed tasks. They have adopted these approaches instead of relying on the play-based, centre-based programs that, we know, help children to thrive.

A focus on worksheets and teacher-directed tasks overlooks the reality that, for children, play is their work. All play embraces the fact that children's learning is dynamic, messy, and uneven. Play honors the fact that children progress through a series of developmental stages, while teacher-directed worksheet challenges do not — they do not lend themselves to being individualized. Young learners learn best when they are actively engaged, as in play. They learn by doing.

Children engage in different kinds of play — self-directed, organizational, and educational — and taking part only in self-directed play and organizational play is not enough for them. When engaged in *self-directed* play such as building a fort in the basement, children create the structure and the rules for the activity. In *organizational* play in the local playground — for example, a soccer game — children are provided with the rules and structure. In *educational* play, in the Kindergarten classroom, the teacher structures the environment to ensure that optimal learning will take place. We have found that the creation of several learning centres is the best way to achieve this.

In developing this book, our intent has been to provide many practical ideas that we have successfully used to infuse literacy activities into the traditional centres of our Kindergarten classrooms: these include the Sand, Water, and Construction centres. We want to support teachers as they move beyond worksheets. Teachers already using a centres approach will find ideas to enhance literacy learning in their Kindergarten classrooms. We will also offer answers to such questions as these: "How do children learn to read and write while playing?" "How do teachers structure the play so that children of all backgrounds and abilities can meet with success?" "What kind of environment needs to be created so that children will be excited about reading and writing?" "How does one teacher manage all these different interests and developmental levels?" These are all questions that reflective practitioners ask in their quest to provide effective programs for young learners.

Educational Play: Social Aspects

Children approach educational play in different ways. While playing, some children concentrate on their own activity, having no social interaction with their peers or teachers (solitary play). Others play side by side, sharing the space, but using their own activity with their own materials (parallel play). Still others share materials and work in concert with their peers, planning together, sharing the thinking, doing, and problem-solving (co-operative play).

The Constant in Our Journey as Educators: Play

Our journey as educators has been influenced by many great teachers and educational thinkers. We have learned and grown beside our students, and over the years, we have thoughtfully altered our programs to better serve their changing needs. Despite these changes, our basic philosophy of "Play" has remained the same. What is different is that, over time, we have more fully recognized the relationship between play and literacy. The chart below briefly outlines our journey.

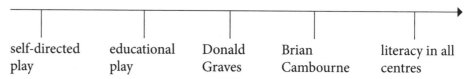

self-directed play | educational play | Donald Graves | Brian Cambourne | literacy in all centres

Self-directed play

At the beginning of our careers, our Kindergartens focused on self-directed play. Our teaching emphasis was on children having a positive beginning to school and building a good attitude and a strong foundation for later learning. We provided the children with a variety of experiences and activities, for example, drawing and painting, as well as using building toys, stacking toys, puzzles, bin toys (Brio railroad set), a sandbox with a pail and shovel, a water table with boats, and a dollhouse. The children were free to follow their own learning while we circulated throughout the classroom and talked with the children about their play. There was little evidence of print in the environment, and we read to the children only at Storytime.

The emphasis was on expanding the children's oral language and listening skills. The children worked independently or in small groups at activities of their own choosing where they were encouraged to talk, listen, describe, question, and co-operate. Our role was to respond to the children's interests and questions — we rarely intruded into the play. The children were free to visit all areas in an unstructured manner. The books we read to them were generally stories for enjoyment; rarely were they non-fiction, poetry, or Big Books. Our selections were unconnected to the children's play.

At this time, some of our colleagues used a different strategy. They would assign a teacher-directed task for all the children to complete during a "work" period. When the children had completed this "work," they were free to play with toys in a self-directed manner. They thereby gained a "play" period.

Moving towards educational play

As we continued to reflect on our practice, we realized we needed to modify our programs so that they better reflected educational play. We needed to take a more active role in structuring the play. At this time, we adopted a centres approach to expand the children's experiences in the classroom. For example, at the sandbox, we added a table or shelf that held additional props to extend the children's play and discovery (e.g., measuring cups, moulds, and scales). We also made these additions to the Water centre and to the House centre.

At this time in our practice, we would create Interest centres, usually one at a time. Each lasted for as long as it held student interest, which could be for a few days or weeks. We introduced a variety of materials related to a particular interest the children had expressed. For example, if the children showed an interest in turtles, we would gather a turtle puzzle, a real turtle, and a few books about turtles and then encourage children to paint, draw, or make their versions of turtles at the Visual Arts centre. Other children could refer to the materials from the Interest centre table to make habitats in the Sand centre. Our goal at the Interest centre was to help children make connections between real objects (concrete), pictures and models (semi-abstract), and books (abstract). We did this because the children were at many different stages of development and this practice honored all their levels.

As interest grew and more questions arose, the Interest centre sometimes transformed into something of broader context. For example, the turtle interest could expand into a focus on ponds. More sensory, concrete, semi-abstract, and abstract materials would then be added. As a result, many more children found an aspect of the topic to be excited about. With this experiential educational play approach, the children were now able to make more meaningful connections to their learning and relate it to their own experiences.

In responding to an interest that the children had expressed, we rejected a manner of teaching adopted by some of our colleagues: providing pre-cut materials for prescribed and teacher-directed themes, for example, a paper plate, green paint, and googly eyes for a turtle. We preferred to introduce to the Visual Arts centre a wide range of materials that supported an interest, for example, cotton batten for snow and feathers for birds. We did this because we thought that the children, not the teacher, should do the thinking, planning, and problem solving. We recognized that by doing most of the work, the teacher would be setting up some children to fail, as not all were at the developmental level that allowed them to successfully reproduce a teacher's model.

We wrote *for* the children and we read *for* them. We read aloud stories about the interest, for example, dinosaurs. We then added these stories to the Reading centre. Children also wanted to tell their own stories. We acted as scribes, writing out the captions and stories they dictated to us.

At this time, we did not yet see the centres in the room as a rich source of literacy learning. Instead, we viewed the learning at the centres as an opportunity for the children to experience new ideas, expand their knowledge, make connections, and work co-operatively rather than in an isolated and parallel manner. We still concentrated on oral language and listening skills to the exclusion of reading and writing — there was little or no print in the environment.

Finding support in the work of Donald Graves

The time came when we recognized that reading and writing instruction could no longer be reserved for Grade 1. We needed to recognize the varying competencies of four and five year-olds when they entered school. Some children came to school already reading, while others were still struggling to recognize their own names or letters of the alphabet. For those children who were capable of storytelling, we acted as a scribe, writing down dictated stories about their drawings and paintings. We encouraged the children to read their own compositions. As the children became aware of print and showed an interest in reading relevant words such as *mommy, daddy, dog,* and *cat,* we wrote these words on individual cards, creating a personal word box. We asked them to use these words to fill in any blanks and complete their dictated stories — they enjoyed "reading" these stories. Becoming frustrated by the lack of easy-to-read, repetitive pattern books, we began to make our own class booklets and charts.

The work of Donald Graves came to influence our thinking. Graves argued that children went through a series of developmental stages as they learned to write. He suggested that, given the opportunity to write, children would naturally write. We agreed that many children had a wealth of understanding about environmental print long before they came to school. Many knew and read their street sign, a Stop sign, and the names of their mom, dad, and siblings.

Consequently, we introduced a Drawing/Writing centre and began to encourage the children to write for themselves. We provided alphabet cards for reference and individual direct instruction at the centre. We encouraged the children to write on topics of their choice and to add meaningful captions on their work. When conferencing with the children, we were astounded by how many of them could write and how much they could compose. Their writing flourished, and they willingly and enthusiastically read aloud their work. At that time, the literacy learning in our classrooms began to include not only listening and speaking but reading and writing, too.

The impact of Brian Cambourne's work

Our Kindergarten programs grew and changed again when we were introduced to Brian Cambourne's work in *The Whole Story*.

Cambourne identified significant conditions that were present when children were successfully learning to talk. He taught us that learners require opportunity, demonstration, choice, instruction, practice, timely feedback, and a chance to make and learn from mistakes. We understood the importance of the learner taking responsibility for the learning, but more significantly, we learned the importance of the learner seeing the need for the learning.

Engagement is the culmination of all Cambourne's conditions of learning. Children become truly engaged in their learning when all the conditions are present. The following are Cambourne's seven conditions:

1. **Responsibility:** Encourage children to take responsibility and ownership for their own learning by making choices and decisions about their work and learning.
2. **Immersion:** Immerse children in a print-rich environment full of meaningful literacy materials and experiences.
3. **Expectation:** Expect that all children can and will succeed.
4. **Demonstration:** Provide demonstrations to help ensure that children have many opportunities to experience a variety of instructional techniques, such as modelling, observing, and direct instruction, as well as referring to books and other materials for information (e.g., a newspaper to find a movie).
5. **Use and Practice:** Provide regular opportunities for students to use their developing skills. Doing so makes improvement and consolidation possible.
6. **Approximation:** Since children have different abilities and skills, all their efforts are respected and encouraged. Children are invited to take risks, to "have a go," to move towards increasingly accurate conventions and skills. They are not all expected to do the same thing at the same time. Differences are expected and do not stand out for critical evaluation or comparison.
7. **Feedback/Positive Response:** Offer encouragement so that developing learners will continue to take risks and make further attempts with the learning. This encouragement might include oral comments, written messages, or constructive suggestions that will provide immediate incentive for children to keep striving.

Literacy in all the centres

As we reflected on Cambourne's work, we saw how his principles of learning could apply to *all* learning and that they would be valuable in creating Kindergarten classrooms with a strong literacy focus. We were excited by the fact that we could easily integrate Cambourne's learning conditions into our play-based Kindergarten programs. Into every centre in the classroom, we infused a wide range of literacy experiences, drawing upon books, photographs, authentic artifacts, and recording materials. We began to link our read-aloud times, Shared Reading times, Shared Writing times, and Borrow-a-Book program to the work at the centres.

We developed extensions at the permanent centres. These were based on our observations of what the children expressed interest in as they played. For example, a child might bring in a picture of a new baby, and many children in the class might begin to talk about their siblings. This occasion could lead to the Home/Dramatic Play centre being turned into a nursery in a hospital. Of course, not all the children were expected to work at any given extension. Many still followed their own interests and projects. However, when the extension came from the children and ownership was taken, other children often became excited about the new props and additions.

We found that the content of an extension did not really matter. All content offers opportunities for the development of literacy skills (listening, describing, questioning, sharing, viewing, retelling, reflecting, relating, and recording). What is key is that the children find relevance in the learning and that the teacher provides a variety of materials and experiences that honor their developmental levels, for example,

- concrete materials (e.g., a real apple to represent an apple) for children in the manipulative stage
- semi-abstract materials (e.g., pictures, photographs, and models) for children in the representational stage
- abstract materials (e.g., texts, CDs, and charts) for children in the abstract stage

Thanks to our understanding of Cambourne's perspective, and the need to make literacy learning relevant, the Kindergarten environment had become rich in literacy learning.

The Limitations of Worksheets

By infusing literacy activities into every facet of our program, we were able to demonstrate to parents, other teachers, and administrators that we had no need to resort to worksheets to help children develop their literacy skills.

We recommend a viable alternative to worksheets: either blank sheets or templates. Worksheets, either commercially purchased or teacher-made, paper-and-pencil assignments, often include many extraneous instructions, illustrations, and titles. They typically require the learner to connect ideas, complete a blank, circle the correct answer, copy the text, or match images and letters. In contrast, teachers can make use of blank pieces of paper or templates, which are bridges between blank sheets and worksheets. A template has an organized format designed by the teacher and provides the children with the opportunity to add their ideas and knowledge to the organizer (e.g., a T-chart, a tally, a word web). (See Appendix A: Ways to Record Ideas.)

When we examined the practice of using worksheets versus blank sheets or templates, we found the following comparison:

Worksheet	Blank Piece of Paper *or* Template
Provides a limited opportunity for diagnosis to guide future teaching. (For example: If the child is required only to circle all the *c*s, then the child's knowledge of vowels cannot be diagnosed.)	Provides a broader opportunity for diagnosis to guide future teaching. (For example: If the child writes, "I LV CTS," then the teacher knows that the next step in this child's learning might include a vowel mini-lesson.)
Generally focuses on only one skill (e.g., connecting pictures with letters or circling one word or filling in a blank).	Focuses on a variety of skills and knowledge (e.g., practising spacing, making connections with all of the sound symbols, focusing on directionality of print).
Driven by the teacher. (For example: The teacher makes a sheet where children must connect the picture of a cat with the letter *c*.)	Driven by the learner. (For example: The learner has the opportunity to solve a problem and make decisions.)
The teacher does the thinking, problem solving, and most of the work — the learner is passive.	The student does all the thinking, problem solving, and work, and is actively engaged in the learning process.
Narrow, since everyone does the same task and generally there is only one right answer and the rest of the responses are wrong. Too difficult for some; too easy for others.	Differentiated, so everyone can work at their own level and, therefore, appropriate for all.
Boring for some and interesting for only a few.	Interesting, challenging, and relevant to all.
Addresses one developmental level.	Addresses many different levels as the task can be approached by children of different abilities (e.g., a string of letters, captions, or sentences)
Often requires only one response.	Invites multiple responses.
Demonstrates limited picture of child's knowledge.	Demonstrates a broad picture of the child's individual skills.
Provides limited opportunities for oral language.	Provides a myriad of opportunities for oral language.

Allows no ownership.	Allows ownership because the content is the children's choice.
Often involves copying teacher's work (e.g., printing letter *b* over and over again).	Involves practising many literacy skills (e.g., letter formation, sound–symbol relationship, purpose for writing).
Closed.	Open-ended.
Learner works alone.	Learner can work collaboratively.
Often requires the adult to read/reread the instructions. Directions are often unclear, requiring interpretation or instructions (For example: Illustrations are often confusing — an alligator or a crocodile?)	Requires less adult assistance. The children create any illustrations that are necessary.
Can't be extended. When the child is finished, there is nothing left to do but perhaps color on the back of the sheet.	Can be extended.
Takes a short time to complete.	Requires more focus and attention; therefore, the child can spend as long as is necessary to complete the task appropriately.

Thus, we saw worksheets as having limited use for diagnosing future teaching points and developing individual literacy skills — these fit into a more teacher-directed Kindergarten program. By contrast, templates or blank sheets provided more opportunity for differentiated response and instruction. They fit well into a play-based, centre-based Kindergarten program.

The chapters that follow offer specific, open-ended literacy activities, titles of effective books to share with children, names of wonderful authors to introduce to the class, and suggestions for useful templates, games, and materials. All of the literacy opportunities are presented as a richer alternative to worksheets. This book also identifies questions to consider when setting up each learning centre. Finally, it outlines developmental mileposts to guide teacher observations and document the progress of the children at play.

Teachers can move beyond the limits of worksheets and pre-cut art projects to foster meaningful learning. They can honor the children's individual developmental levels and their need to learn through play. This book, based on much seasoned experience and reflective practice, will help teachers do that successfully.

1

Creating the Learning Environment

The environment is paramount to a successful Kindergarten literacy program. An optimum environment is one that promotes shared responsibility between the teacher and the children. Such an environment provides a stimulating, positive climate and takes into account learning styles, decision-making process, timetable, physical organization, evaluation techniques, and the varying roles of the participants. Creating such an environment also involves considering space for instruction both individual and whole group, including demonstrations, minilessons, and conferences that suit the development of the students. As a result of these many concerns, we continually ask ourselves the following key questions:

- What organizational structure will work best?
- How will the classroom operate?
- How will we timetable to ensure the most efficient use of teacher and student time?
- What learning is taking place and who is doing the work?
- If we adopt learning centres as our organizational structure, how do we plan them in order to maximize learning for all children?

We address these questions in this chapter and explore the workings of various learning centres in chapters 3 to 9.

An Organizational Structure That Works: Learning Centres

If children are to develop new skills, knowledge, and attitudes, teachers need to establish a non-threatening atmosphere where risk taking is encouraged. We found that the most effective way to create this was to establish an atmosphere that featured permanent and temporary learning centres complemented by small- and large-group teaching and learning sessions.

Organizing activities through learning centres helps ensure that children have the space that they require. Since isolated desks inhibit collaborative learning and prevent easy access to learning activities, we preferred to use circular tables which invite more collaborative learning. Every child cannot have a personal workspace, as well as access to learning centres. What children do need is a place to store their personal treasures — we found individual cubbies a good way to provide this space. Children need space to actively engage, explore, design, construct, communicate, and learn together.

The following centres are a must in any Kindergarten classroom:

- Drawing/Writing (including a computer)
- Reading (including a listening station)
- Visual Arts
- Home/Dramatic Play

- Water
- Sand
- Construction
- Celebration and Special Event (special focus)

All centres provide learning opportunities for children to acquire the skills, knowledge, and attitudes that educational authorities generally prescribe. We learned that the major subject areas of the curriculum could be integrated into these centres. This organization allowed children to learn in small groups, large groups, or individually, at a variety of activities.

Negotiating centre choice

For real learning to take place, children need to take ownership and select the activities, but under certain conditions.

When introducing each centre, we discussed with the children how many people they thought could safely and comfortably play there. For example, at the Home/Dramatic Play centre, we decided that three children would be an optimum number. A pictorial or written sign was placed in each centre for a reminder.

We began every activity period by asking each of the children where they preferred to start or continue their work. As children chose the centre where they wanted to work, we informed the others in the group that there was now room for one or two more participants before that centre was full. However, if after careful tracking, we found that some children repeatedly chose the same narrow range of activities, then we stepped in and limited or extended these choices. We would honor their initial choice but make a point to inform them that they would be working at another activity of our choice later in the activity period.

Teacher-directed versus child-chosen tasks

Some teachers have difficulty trusting children's choices and so they make task decisions for them. They rotate children through a variety of learning experiences at centres and assign teacher-directed tasks. "Today, you must paint a picture of an apple for the apple tree."

Overemphasis on teacher-directed tasks, especially paper-and-pencil ones, is counterproductive. It does not respect children's differing developmental levels or interests. Nor does it allow for the key learning conditions of ownership, responsibility, relevance, and varied expectation. For example, a worksheet that requires the children to merely circle all the pictures whose object names begin in the same way is limited compared to when a teacher asks children to use their knowledge of sound–symbol relationships to write a caption for their illustration. When creating tasks, we have found it helpful to ask ourselves these questions: "Who is doing most of the thinking and learning? Is it the children — or the teacher?" If the answer is the teacher, then the activity needs to be altered to promote problem solving on the part of the children.

Some of our colleagues instituted centres but preferred to take a total-class theme approach involving all the centres. The children were all expected to take part in prescribed thematic activities, for example, tracing and coloring a maple leaf for Fall. We found such teacher-directed activities served only to frustrate some and bore others, as they had no ownership of them. Instead, we encouraged the children to follow their own interests and draw and write about relevant topics, for example, making a picture of a new pet, a recent birthday, or weekend

The Celebration and Special Event centre may give temporary focus to a celebration or special event such as Halloween, Hanukkah, or Chinese New Year.

Sample Distribution of Children at Centres

During the Literacy and the Arts time
3 in the Home/Dramatic Play centre
4 in the Reading centre (2 at the listening station; 2 reading)
4 in the Visual Arts centre
2 at the Celebration centre
7 at the Drawing/Writing centre (2 on the computer; 5 using the other materials)

During the Literacy and Math, Science, and Technology time
3 in the Sand centre
3 in the Water centre
3 in big blocks (an area within the Construction centre)
9 in the Construction centre (basically, using all available tables or Plexiglas)
2 on the computer (using a math-related program)

A Matter of Strategy

Deciding which children to ask next is governed by these priorities:
1. Do the children have work to finish?
2. Do you as teacher want to work with the children?
Choice then becomes random. Sometimes, if children always choose the same activity, you may want to wait until that centre is filled before calling their names.

trip to the amusement park. The children were more engaged and motivated to write and draw when they selected a topic that was important to them.

The nature of centre materials

Even such centres as Sand and Water benefit from books, pictures, and puzzles that reflect the literacy extensions. It is recommended that the following types of materials and resources be embedded in all centres in the classroom:

- concrete/real objects from different cultures (e.g., woks in the House centre)
- semi-abstract materials (e.g., pictures, posters, models)
- abstract materials (e.g., books, videos, CDs, activities, games, puzzles)
- bias-free materials (e.g., books that reflect a variety of races, cultures, and gender roles)
- tables and shelves
- a bulletin board to display photographs, pictures, posters, and children's work
- resources to extend the inquiries and projects (e.g., magnifying glasses, scales, and measurement tapes)
- writing materials (e.g., pencils, markers, graph paper, clipboard)

Balancing demands for space

The design and configuration of each classroom present challenges and limitations in terms of space and equipment. As we initially set up a physical environment, we considered the need for the following:

- easy access to the materials (Children should be able to independently get materials out and put them away.)
- quiet places for students who need them
- areas for water/sand activities
- space for small-group activities
- a place for everyone to gather
- space allowing traffic flow
- a conference area or table
- a place for the children to keep their coats and personal treasures

This room layout has worked well for us.

Here is a flexible and efficient layout for a classroom with key learning centres. The availability of electrical outlets for the computer and listening station, as well as the location of the water supply, often dictates where individual centres are placed. It is important to keep any computers away from the water.

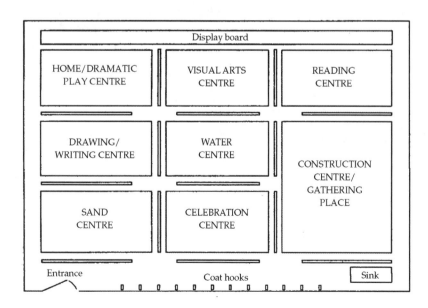

Questions about setting up a classroom with centres

There is no one right way to set up a Kindergarten classroom but considering the following questions will provide successful options.

- How will you arrange the furniture (desks or tables) to accommodate the necessary centre?
- Where will the children keep their personal belongings? (Perhaps in a box, in a basket, or in a cubby.)
- Where will storage containers be kept? (Choices include shelves or an open cupboard.)
- When will new permanent centres be added? (It's best to do so when the other centres are running smoothly and to add the centres one at a time so they can be introduced properly.)
- Where will the shared supplies be kept? (They can be kept at each centre or at a separate communal supplies centre.)
- Where will the children gather for a story, a song, Shared Reading sessions, Shared Writing time, and discussion? (The carpet and the teacher' chair are common choices.)
- What is needed at the gathering place? (You may want to use a chair, an easel, a carpet, a whiteboard, a pocket chart, a chalkboard, and a SMART Board.)
- Where will you, as teacher, conference with individuals and small groups? (You may consider meeting on the carpet, at your chair, or at a table.)
- Which centres require special equipment or space? (These may include the Home, Sand, Water, and Construction centres.)
- Where will finished work be stored? (Perhaps in a bin or on a table.)
- Where will unfinished work be stored? (Consider putting it in work folders, on a separate table, or in a bin.)

The Importance of Routines

Human beings thrive on routine and expectation. For children, specifically, routine provides a safe and predictable environment. The centres in our classrooms were more successful when routines were explicit and meaningful.

Where practical, children in our Kindergartens had some input and ownership in modifying the routines. For example, they might say, "The Water centre is too crowded — maybe two people instead of three should go there." They also helped to monitor the success of the routines and made suggestions for changes where necessary during regularly held classroom discussions. Since the classroom is for the children, it is important for the orchestration of the environment to involve them as much as possible.

Routines, if they are to succeed, must be carefully introduced to the children. This process usually takes several weeks accompanied by frequent reminders. Many mini-lessons are needed to remind the children of the expectations and to reinforce the process. One routine that typically needs constant reminders is tidy up in the Home/Dramatic Play centre. Children need to be reminded to put the materials used back into their labelled bins (e.g., baby clothes in one drawer and pots and pans in the appropriate labelled space under the stove).

Our goal was for children to use the centres independently, assuming responsibility for many for the housekeeping chores in the busy Kindergarten classroom. We, as teachers, were then able to concentrate on the more important

If a routine is not working, it is always wise to examine what is causing it to break down. Reflection might include addressing such questions as these:
Does getting the children to tidy up take a long time?
Should tidy up at some of the centres be started before others? (The Construction and Water centres are candidates.)
Would a warning signal be useful?
Is enough time allotted?
Considering these questions will help improve the success of classroom routines.

tasks, including demonstrating, coaching, facilitating, listening, questioning, supporting, and offering feedback.

Questions to consider when developing routines for the centres

Be sure to consider these key questions when in the midst of developing routines for the successful use of centres:

- How many children can work safely at each centre?
- How will the children know how many of them can work at each centre? (Consider using a sign, a picture, or a sign-up sheet.)
- What supplies will be needed?
- Where will the supplies be stored? (At a central supply depot or in baskets at each centre.)
- Who will be responsible for replenishing the consumable supplies? (Either the teacher or the children who serve as monitors can be responsible.)
- What materials will be needed for an efficient and effective tidy up?
- How will the children know who is responsible? (Options include use of a monitors' chart or assignment of tasks by the teacher or whoever works at the centre each day.)
- How will the children know to stop and listen? (You may want to use a bell, a flick of the lights, or a song.)

Effective Timetables

How many centres are open at a time depends on the comfort level and personal choices of the teacher. Many experienced teachers who use centres to organize a Kindergarten have all of the centres open during a work period. Some teachers have all centres open but choose a specific focus for their interactions with the children. They might think, for example, "Today I plan to visit the Water centre and help the children at the Drawing/Writing centre to label their pictures." Other teachers, however, struggle when all the centres are open at the same time. With such a wide selection of activities and children at different developmental levels, they report that they cannot spend as much time as they need to in order to support children's learning. They are equally uncomfortable with the old work-and-play periods in which children complete teacher-directed tasks first and then, time permitting, select activities that interest them.

Divided activity times

In our Kindergarten classrooms, we achieved a more manageable focus by introducing two distinct activity periods. One period focused on reading, writing, and the arts; the other focused on math, science, and technology. The activity period for reading, writing, and the arts featured learning centres such as these:

- Reading centre
- Drawing/Writing centre
- Home/Dramatic Play centre
- Visual Arts centre
- Celebration and Special Event centre (temporary)

The period that focused on math, science, and technology activities featured learning centres such as these:

- Construction centre
- Sand centre
- Water centre

Since all learning with young children is so integrated, we infused literacy into all of these centres, using oral and written language to refer to, describe, and record children's structures and discoveries.

We found that with this divided timetable, we could spend quality time at each centre and that both we and the children gained a clear focus. We had the time to meaningfully conference with the children, demonstrate a new skill one on one, and regularly offer timely feedback. We had more time to introduce, support, and reinforce the critical routines of only a few centres, instead of all the centres in the room. We found we could plan to spend more time at each of the centres observing, modelling, and extending the learning. We could use our time more effectively: for example, early in the year at the Drawing/Writing centre, we might teach the children how to print their own names. When all of the activities were open at the same time, spending quality time at each centre was difficult.

With the divided focus organization, time is spent equally in all areas of the curriculum. Just as time is spent helping children write their own names or signs, it is also spent helping children to pour and measure with increasing accuracy. In such an organization, our behavior makes it explicit that all the learning centres are valued equally. In addition, children spend quality time and have experiences in all areas of the curriculum.

Working with variations in scheduling

There is a great deal of variation in scheduling Kindergarten programs. In some jurisdictions, Kindergarten students come to school all day every day for an all-day Kindergarten program. Others come to school for half-day Kindergarten programs. In still others where busing exists, the children come to school all day for two days one week and three days the next week.

The goal in any Kindergarten timetable is to structure it so that there are large blocks of uninterrupted time for the children and teacher to become engaged in meaningful learning at the various centres. Kindergarten teachers usually prefer to have release teachers teach music or drama, physical education, and computer or library skills rather than try to implement one of the activity periods. Other learning experiences such as physical education, music, read-aloud, Shared Reading and Writing demonstrations, computer/library instruction, outdoor play, and even snack must, however, be considered and incorporated when finalizing a timetable. All these experiences need to be provided within the context of teachers' contractual preparation release time.

All-day Kindergarten timetable

9:00	Entrance, Cloakroom, Book Exchange, Attendance
9:05–9:15	Personal Book Time
9:15–9:30	Gathering and Discussion or Story or Shared Reading or Shared Writing
9:30–10:30	Literacy and the Arts Activity Period: Snack Time is during this time.
10:30–10:45	Tidy Up, Culmination, Celebration
10:45–11:30	Physical Education, Music, Library, or Buddy Reading
11:30	Dismissal for Lunch

New Kindergarten teachers often overlook math, science, and technology activities such as building with big blocks and construction materials in favor of the reading and writing activities. Doing this signifies a lost opportunity to infuse literacy extensions into the rest of the classroom.

Lunch

12:30–12:35	Entrance, Cloakroom, Gathering
12:35–1:00	Story, Large-Group Shared Reading or Writing Time with a focus on math, science, and technology
1:00–2:00	Math, Science, and Technology Activity Period: Snack Time is during this time.
2:00–2:15	Tidy Up, Culmination, Celebration
2:15–2:45	Story, Drama/Movement, or Outdoor Play
2:45–3:00	Dismissal

Half-day Kindergarten timetable

9:00	Entrance, Cloakroom, Book Exchange, Attendance
9:05–9:15	Gathering on the carpet; Private time with a book
9:15–9:30	Discussion, Shared Reading or Writing, Story
9:30–10:15	Literacy and the Arts Activity Period
10:15–10:30	Tidy Up, Celebration
10:30–10:45	Music, Drama, or Movement
10:45–11:15	Literacy and Math, Science, and Technology Activity Period
11:15–11:30	Celebration and Culmination
11:30	Dismissal

Teachers are encouraged to alternate the Literacy and the Arts activity period and the Literacy and Math, Science, and Technology period every other day to equalize the time available and recognize the importance of each activity period.

The First Day of School

The first day of school is a significant day in the lives of young children. Many children eagerly enter school looking forward to the experiences that older siblings and neighborhood friends have shared. For others, who have never left the security of their homes, the change can be difficult. They are often nervous, hesitant, even fearful. For those who do not speak English at home, entering school can be even more challenging. We as teachers must take care to structure the first day, so that the transition from home to school is smooth and positive.

On the first day of school, everything is new and unfamiliar to the children. A large Kindergarten classroom can seem daunting to them. Having the teacher take many opportunities throughout the day to introduce the routines and expectations to the children will help allay children's concerns.

We always began the first day by following the divided activity period schedule. We were careful to introduce and open only some of the centres, thereby focusing the children's attention and learning.

The day began with the children entering the classroom and looking for their nametags on the conferencing table, thereby giving the teacher an initial understanding of the children's comfort in the room and their literacy skills. The children would be invited to place their personal items on a hook or in a cubby and then gather on the carpet and look at a book from the bin in the middle of the carpet.

Sometimes, parents stayed or some children shed a few tears. In this case, the children would sometimes look around the classroom, examining each centre. When this happened, we would dim the lights to attract the attention of the children and the parents, and then invite the children to say goodbye to their parents and gather on the carpet to begin our first day together.

On the carpet, we would introduce ourselves by reading a homemade book with a title such as "Meet Mrs. Flemington." We recommend including about 10 points and using simple, repetitive text that introduces the teacher to the class:

I love to snow ski.
I love my family.
I love going to the park.

Each one-line strip of text can be produced on the computer and glued down below a related photo or photos. For example, in "Meet Mrs. Flemington," there is a photo of teacher and child in a pool above the line "I love swimming." The photo is a good-sized 18 cm by 20.5 cm (7 by 8 inches).

Following this read-aloud, we would invite the children to raise a hand and orally share information about themselves. Typically, we ask about three questions that mirror text from the teacher book. If the teacher wrote, "I love chocolate chip cookies," a question to ask might be, "What do you love to eat?"

We would then enthusiastically tell the children that we would be having fun together and learning so many new and exciting things. In preparation we would make a simple chart listing all the activities in the classroom and place photographs beside the name of each centre. We would read this chart to the children and then quickly tour the children around the classroom, pointing out the Reading centre, Drawing/Writing centre, Home/Dramatic Play centre, Construction centre, Sand centre, Water centre, and Visual Arts centre. (These centres would all be set up, but introduced and opened gradually over a few weeks.)

We used this time to briefly demonstrate the routines and procedures at these centres. For example, we drew attention to pictorial signs indicating how many children could work at a particular centre. We also provided the appropriate amount of materials, such as three aprons at the Water centre and three plastic construction hats for use with big blocks at the Construction centre. We pointed out where the materials were kept and emphasized how they were to be returned to their own marked place at tidy-up time. We spoke to the children about the divided activity time and helped them understand that some centres would sometimes be closed.

We were then ready to begin our first activity time in reading, writing, and visual arts. We told the children that the Reading centre, Drawing/Writing centre, a temporary Puzzle Table, and the Visual Arts centre, featuring playdough, were all open, and we invited the children to select a place in the room to work. Since we gave each child a personal drawing and writing book (see Chapter 3), we invited some to illustrate the cover of their book at the Drawing/Writing centre.

It may seem like only a few activities for the first day, but starting slowly helped to build a strong foundation for routines and expectations. Limiting choices created a calm and focused environment.

After about half an hour of Reading, Writing, and Visual Arts activity time, we demonstrated the stop work signal by dimming the lights and directing the children to stop and listen. We had the children tidy up and gather on the carpet. We celebrated the learning by asking several children to share the illustrations that they had done in their drawing and writing books. The teacher, as well as the audience of children, would then make comments and suggestions, for example, "I like how you used so many colors on your tree — it looks like Fall."

To create the reusable book of introduction, it works well to use colored construction paper in 46 cm by 30.5 cm spreads (18 by 12 inches, each page 9 inches across), to show text and photos on right-side pages only, and to staple the spreads about five times through the centre fold.

Here is the cover of one child's personal drawing and writing book. The child, Mei, said, "I made a picture and a ruler and a pencil, and lots of writing at the bottom."

Establishing a stop work signal is critical as subsequent learning hinges on the teacher being able to gain the children's attention instantly.

We then invited the children to eat their snacks from home while we read aloud *I Can Build* by Shiego Watanabe. In this book, bears use blocks to build a house and it falls repeatedly, but they persevere and problem-solve to succeed. The theme of this book led into the next activity period.

The children took part in an abbreviated Math, Science, and Technology activity period. Giving each child a bin, we introduced the children to the construction materials and invited them to build at a table or on the carpet. During this activity period, we circulated throughout the room, talking with the children, reinforcing the routines, and praising all the children for their efforts. After the children had built for about a half-hour, we demonstrated the tidy-up routine, which involved quietly placing a set of materials back into a bin and returning the bin to its marked place in the Construction centre.

The children then gathered on the carpet. There, the class discussed the day's events, heard a story about school such as *Spot Goes to School* by Eric Hill, chanted a simple poem, or sang a few songs familiar to the children.

The first few weeks

The first few days are a time to get to know the children, talk with them about their interests, observe and note their developmental levels, and read many stories to add to the Reading centre. Most important, we reinforced the routines: it is impossible to work with a small group of children if the others in the room cannot work independently.

Once the children understood and followed the routines, we added other centres one at a time. Next, we usually introduced painting at the Visual Arts centre and then introduced the Sand centre, the Water centre, and big blocks at the Construction centre. We took our time, introducing each of these centres with a story (see the following chapters for some specific ideas of introduction).

Over time, we developed the number and nature of learning centres. During these first few weeks, as we noted children's developmental levels and interests, we began to add materials to the permanent centres. For example, if the children talked about picking apples, then we added vegetable and fruit models to the Home/Dramatic Play centre. Once all the permanent centres were well established, we infused a literacy extension into one of them. We might, for example, transform the Home/Dramatic Play centre into a fruit and vegetable store.

The Basis of Success

In summary, successful Kindergarten classrooms rely on careful consideration being given to classroom organization, routines, and timetables. They also call on teachers to spend time thinking about the centres, what learning they expect to occur, what conditions need to be present for literacy learning to take place, what materials will support this learning, and what routines are particularly necessary to ensure that the children can use the centres independently.

Chapters 3 through 9 discuss the main learning centres, putting an emphasis on literacy activities. They offer a rationale for each centre, lists of materials that encourage literacy learning, questions that reflective practitioners might ask, developmental mileposts to help guide teacher observations, and specific open-ended literacy activities that have proven successful. First though, Chapter 2 outlines literacy-related classroom activities that complement centre play.

2

Whole-Class Literacy Experiences

In a play-based, child-centred Kindergarten, many literacy experiences occur at the permanent learning centres, such as the Drawing/Writing centre and even the Sand and Construction centres. At the various centres, the children develop their abilities to think, communicate, problem-solve, listen, read, write and work co-operatively and collaboratively.

In addition to the learning at these centres, many other rich literacy experiences are provided in the Kindergarten program. Some of these activities occur in the large-group gathering times, some work best with small groups, and others are more individualized. In this chapter, we outline various literacy activities that complement and reinforce what happens at these centres.

Gathering Times as an Anchor

Of primary importance to the smooth and effective functioning of the centres are the Gathering Times on the carpet. These times provide an anchor which supports and fosters successful learning in each of the learning centres. Since the children have different attention spans, different speaking and listening skills and interests, these meetings are short and occur frequently at a variety of times. They may occur at the beginning of the day, between activity times, and at the end of the day.

Gathering Times serve a variety of purposes, many related to literacy building.

- Some purposes relate to classroom management. The teacher can take attendance, introduce a new routine, or reinforce the specific expectations for tidy-up time, for example, where to put unfinished work.
- Gathering Times allow the teacher to introduce new things: to play a new game, to teach a new song or poem.
- They permit the enjoyment of a read-aloud of children's literature, non-fiction, or poetry, as well as personal quiet time with a book.
- They are occasions on which children can engage in formal discussions, play familiar and story character roles, take part in listening memory games, and sing new and familiar songs.
- Children can participate in Shared Reading experiences using a Daily Message, Big Book, chart, poem, rhyme, or song; they can also have Shared Writing experiences, contributing to the creation of a chart, letter, or list.
- On the carpet after an activity time, the class can meet to celebrate and share the children's learning.

Small-group opportunities

On some occasions, the teacher might choose to meet with a small group of children on the carpet. These small-group meetings would occur during an activity time in an effort to differentiate instruction. Sometimes, we structured the group so all of the children were at the same developmental level while at other times, we created a group based on interest, for example, the children at the temporary Shoe Store centre needing to know how to list the prices of different shoes. Although we held Shared Reading and Writing sessions with both the whole class and small groups of children, we often found that these times were more meaningful and productive when we worked with small groups. We were better able to manage the group and ensure that all the children were equally involved.

An ebb and flow in groupings

These large- and small-group opportunities provide a stimulating and motivating interplay among the centres. The teacher is able to successfully introduce, demonstrate, teach, reinforce, and celebrate new concepts, skills, and attitudes as well as generate an excitement for learning. In addition, this format allows the children to receive meaningful and immediate responses from the teacher and from their peers. Immersed in such a rich environment, they are able to make real connections that inspire continuous learning. A natural ebb and flow develops as the children and the teacher move from individual and small-group activity to large-group involvement.

All of the activities outlined below could be adapted to small-group and individual conferences. The teacher does this on an ongoing basis when interacting with the children at the various centres during an activity period.

Read-Aloud Sessions

We believe that when teachers take the time to read to children, they help to immerse children in the rich world of literature. They can use this time to introduce the children to a variety of texts, including poetry, expository, and narrative texts. It has been our experience that by listening to stories read or told aloud, the children are motivated to read for themselves. Through exposure to fiction and non-fiction, they are introduced to real reasons for reading.

The selection of materials to be shared in read-aloud sessions is critically important. Sometimes, we invited the children to make selections to share with the class; however, most of the time, we made the selection because we had a specific purpose in mind for this special time. We were careful to ensure that all the materials presented were inclusive and bias free. We made sure that the children in the room saw their own images and those of the broader community.

One favorite was *Cleversticks* by Bernard Ashley. In this book, the main character, Ling Sung, dreads going to school because there are so many things he cannot do. When he discovers that the other children admire his ability to use chopsticks, Ling Sung begins to get excited about going to school.

We read aloud several times a day, using materials for specific purposes.

- We used Big Books such as *Something from Nothing* by Phoebe Gilman to model specific text forms and specific reading skills.
- We used simple pattern and repetitive text, such as *I Went Walking* by Sue Williams, so that after readings, the children would be able to read these

materials independently. Resources such as *Mary Had a Red Dress* or *Henry Wore His Green Sneakers,* both by Merle Peek, also helped to motivate the children to use the patterns from the original text to create their own books.

- We selected particular stories because of their strong storyline, for example, *Rosie's Walk* by Pat Hutchins. Doing this helped the children to retell and sequence order. Often the stories were connected to one of the other centres in the room. *Who Sank the Boat?* by Pamela Allen is a good story to share with the children as they try to get their boats to float at the Water centre.
- We also liked to read a picture book or a fairy tale up to a significant part in the plot and then encourage the children to predict what was going to happen next. We found *Wednesday's Surprise* by Eve Bunting and *Miss Rumphius* by Barbara Cooney to be excellent choices for this activity.
- We selected specific non-fiction materials, such as the Dorling Kindersley books, to model unique features of informational texts: table of contents, glossary, headings, charts, graphs, and more.
- We introduced the children to books that demonstrate a variety of techniques and illustrative materials, including flap books, pop-ups, and borders, in order to expand their use of illustrative techniques in their own writing and publishing.
- We also remembered to choose books that we personally enjoyed in order to promote keen enthusiasm for reading.

For a list of these materials, see Chapter 3: The Drawing/Writing Centre.

Some parents and educators question whether any read-aloud book can satisfy the interests, needs, and levels of all Kindergarten children, but we do not. We believe that stories are not written for any one reading level or age. Good literature, poetry, and non-fiction can appeal to people of all ages and skill levels. For example, many adults enjoy a good children's story such as *Charlotte's Web* by E. B. White or *Dogger* by Shirley Hughes and do so with differing levels of understanding and enjoyment. The same is true of children in any Kindergarten classroom. Nonetheless, we have learned that for the materials to appeal to children, the selection is critical. Randomly picking a book off the shelf to read at the last minute is not enough to motivate or interest Kindergarten children.

We believe that listeners of all ages need to have many experiences with the same book. By doing so, they can read and listen beyond the literal level. Instead of becoming bored, the children become more enthusiastic when they hear a story on several occasions. Each time we read a familiar text, we offered different challenges and insights, so the children could see the value and purpose in rereading it. When revisiting "Jack and the Beanstalk," we might ask, "What might have happened if the giant did not wake up?"

If children and parents are to see the value in rereading, we believe, teachers must be explicit about why revisiting text is important. Shared enjoyment could be one reason — "I just want to read this book again. It is so funny." Through rereadings, children gain a deeper understanding of the author's message and listen at a more interpretive level. By encouraging children to listen to more difficult text than they can read for themselves, we found they were more motivated to choose harder text and to "have a go."

Read-aloud sessions usually take place with the whole group. There are however times when sharing a book with a small group is useful: for example, when a small group of children are planting their bean seeds, a good non-fiction text to read is Dorling Kindersley's *Mini Scientist: In the Garden* by Lisa Burke. These small-group sessions often lead to a rereading with the whole group.

Role of the teacher in read-aloud sessions

Before reading aloud, do some of the following:

- Read the book aloud to yourself so that you are familiar with the text.
- Introduce the children to the book with enthusiasm and express your interest in the text.
- Ask the children to predict why they think you might have selected the book.
- Tell the children why you selected the book (e.g., because you thought the story was funny, it is written by a particular author, it has an intriguing title, or it might help the class learn more about colors).
- Ask the children to look carefully at the cover to get a clue as to what the book may be about.
- Examine the end papers to determine whether they provide any clues about the story.
- Check and discuss the publishing date. (For example: "That was last year," "That was a long time ago," or "That was the year that I was born.")
- Point to the title.
- Draw attention to author name(s).
- Draw attention to illustrator name(s).
- Read and talk about the dedication, if applicable. Ask, "Why do you think the author chose to dedicate this book to that person?"
- Relate and reflect out loud as you refer to various aspects of publication, such as place of publication. (For example: "This Mem Fox book was published in Australia, where the author lives.")

Be mindful that each of these suggestions takes only a few seconds to complete. Nevertheless, you would not use all of them before the reading of every book, so choose only those that are most applicable and relevant to the text and the purpose for reading it.

During the reading, be sure to act on these recommendations:

- Read with expression, emotion, and appropriate voice to emphasize the plot development and characters' feelings.
- Point out significant details in the illustrations or text font.
- Demonstrate the appropriate way to handle a book and turn the pages.
- Pause and look at the children at significant points in the story.
- Pause and make your own predictions. (For example: "I think Miss Rumphius is going to find a way to make the world beautiful too.")
- Pause and ask for their predictions. (For example: "Why do you think the Troll did not eat the littlest Billy Goat Gruff?")
- Be careful not to interrupt the story so much that the flow is harmed.

After the reading, take the opportunity to do the following:

- Pause and wait for the reactions of the children.
- Base any questions on your reason for reading the book, for example, "How was this version of "The Three Little Pigs" different from the other one we read by Paul Galdone?" Try not to spoil the book by asking too many questions.
- Ask children open-ended *why* and *how* questions which require more than a one-word or yes-or-no answer.
- Place the book in the Reading centre or at another appropriate centre, for example, a book about tunnels at the Sand centre, for the children to use throughout the day.
- Research the author or illustrator by searching for information on the Internet alone or doing so with the children using the SMART Board.

Shared Reading Experiences

Children need real reasons to read and write. The work of the permanent centres in the room offers the children many such opportunities. There are also others, as outlined below.

A Daily Message for Sharing

Presenting a Daily Message is one technique we recommend to demonstrate authentic purposes for reading and writing in the Kindergarten classroom. Such a message, often written ahead of time, is short and provides the children with relevant information about new activities or special events. It may appear on a SMART Board or on chart paper clipped to an easel.

A Daily Message can be written at different times of day. Sometimes we wrote one with the children at the beginning of the day, saying, for example, "Today is gym day." Sometimes we wrote them at the end of the day, perhaps printing, "Tomorrow, remember to bring your permission form for the zoo trip." We used pictures and print to differentiate this literacy experience.

The Daily Message technique can be used as both a Shared Reading and Writing experience. If the message is written ahead of time, it is a Shared Reading activity; if the message is written with the children, it is a Shared Writing experience. During Shared Reading times, children can find out about strategies to unlock new words, for example, skipping the word they don't know, continuing reading, and then going back to see whether they can put in a word that makes sense or looking at the first letter for other clues. During Shared Writing times, children can learn new vocabulary — "What word do we need to write next?" They also learn more about sound–symbol relationships — "What letter do you think *zoo* will start with?" They are exposed to simple punctuation rules, for example, "I need to use a period at the end of this sentence."

We introduced many kinds of Shared Reading experiences using Big Books, charts, and more recently, a SMART Board so that the children could more easily see the print. Texts included non-fiction, poetry, chants, songs, and simple pattern books. The materials usually related to the other centres in the room; for example, we might read and chant a simple poem about boats after the Water centre was transformed into a marina.

Sessions such as these allow the teacher to model strategies and reinforce children's knowledge of texts and words. Specific reading strategies to model include using the pictures for clues, rereading the text for clarification, skipping a difficult word, and locating smaller words within larger words. We pointed out simple punctuation, capitalization, and spelling. We also drew their attention to such text features as book title, information about the author and illustrator, and table of contents. We prompted the children to retell the story and predict outcomes. Once the children were familiar with the text, we often created activities to reinforce the vocabulary, perhaps using Post-it notes to create a cloze procedure or framing individual words with our hands to isolate them.

Shared Reading sessions provide opportunities for further literacy activities. We often created collaborative books based on the pattern in a published text. For example, in the book *I Went Walking*, author Sue Williams uses repetitive text to tell the story about farm animals. The children can use the same pattern to retell the story substituting zoo animals. We sometimes role-played familiar parts of a story. For example, "The Three Billy Goats Gruff," "The Three Little Pigs," and "Goldilocks and the Three Bears" are all good stories for dramatizing. We also created story maps (see Appendix A: Ways to Record Ideas) and constructed vocabulary activities such as Bingo, Snap, and Fish games, which were stored with the Big Book at the appropriate centre. (Appendix B: Games describes games such as Snap in more detail.)

The role of the teacher in Shared Reading sessions

The teaching strategies outlined above for read-alouds are also applicable to Shared Reading sessions. The following recommendations are specific to Shared Reading.

Before reading a Big Book or a poem or song printed on chart paper, be sure to prepare the children in these ways.

- Determine why you want to read the book or chart (e.g., to provide enjoyment, to enable chanting of repetitive text, to teach a reading strategy).
- If applicable, draw the attention of the children to illustrations on the cover.
- Ask the children what they think the text might be about.
- As you read the cover, point to and run your finger along the title, the author's name, and the illustrator's name.

During the reading, consider employing these ideas:

- Bring the attention of the children to the top-to-bottom directionality of the text by pointing to the top to begin and the end to finish.
- Draw your finger along the text as you read to indicate the left-to-right direction of the print.
- Comment on punctuation. (For example, ask: "Why do you think the author placed this exclamation mark here?")
- Use your hands to cover words and focus on a few words or repetitive parts.

After the initial reading, you may want to do the following:

- Invite the children to join in at the repetitive parts.
- Since you will be reading the large-print text several times, pause at a few words and invite the children to chime in together.
- Ask for volunteers to read sections of the text.
- Read the Big Book or chart to the group several times over several days.
- Place the book in the Reading centre so that the children can revisit it individually or in small groups.
- Ask the children where in the room you might display a chart, word web, list, poem, or song.
- You can later compile these charts into a Big Book of charts or send home small versions to share with parents/guardians.

Big Books

When using Big Books with Kindergarten students, it is important that the books have these features:

- limited text
- large font
- pattern
- clear, colorful illustrations that are correlated with the text

Try to find Big Books that have multiple copies so that the experience can be extended.

Shared Writing Experiences

Shared Writing experiences provide authentic situations in which to teach the children how to write. By thinking out loud, we showed the children how writers write, how they compose, revise, and edit. We might say: "How can I say that?" "Where will I begin?" "How does that word begin [or end]?" "That doesn't make sense." "I missed out a word — this is how I will put it in." We modelled different spelling strategies, including looking for rhyming words, working from root words, and adding endings.

Shared Writing also permits teachers to introduce different writing forms. We taught the children how to write a letter, record a recipe, and begin a retelling of a fairy tale. We then used the Shared Writing pieces created for other children to read. We encouraged the children to include the pieces in their home-borrowing selections.

Here are some titles we have found useful as jump-offs for children to create collaborative books. The titles all have a strong pattern or rhyme and limited text — a simple format that can be copied and modified by the children. If children in the class used the first title below as a model, they could adapt the pattern to apply to farm animals — "Green Duck, Green Duck, what do you see?" "I see a brown cow looking at me." Many titles have both Big Book and small copy versions that can be made available in multiple copies.

- *Brown Bear, Brown Bear, What Do You See?* by Bill Martin Jr. and Eric Carle
- *Polar Bear, Polar Bear, What Do You Hear?* by Bill Martin Jr. and Eric Carle
- *Cat on the Mat* by Brian Wildsmith
- *K Is for Kiss Good Night* by Jill Sardegna
- *A Dark Dark Tale* by Ruth Brown
- *Where's Spot?* by Eric Hill
- *Coco Can't Wait* by Taro Gomi
- *Ten in a Bed* by Mary Rees

The role of the teacher in Shared Writing sessions

Before the Shared Writing be sure to do the following:

- Clarify the purpose for writing. You might say, "Remember we said that we need to write a letter to thank Corby's mom for helping us with the papier mâché animals yesterday? Let's do that now."
- In terms of content and form, briefly discuss what needs to be included.
- Discuss what types of materials to use (e.g., markers, postcards, letterhead).

During the Shared Writing, plan to do some of the following:

- Think out loud to help children understand something about how a writer thinks. "Where shall I put the title?" or "What do we need to write next?"
- Begin with just a few words; ask the children what letter sounds they hear (e.g., initial consonants). This exercise can be extended as the children become familiar with text and with various sound–symbol relationships.
- Point out some letter formations. You might say, "Move from left to right and begin at the top." You know your students best and are aware of what letters need to be introduced or reinforced.

- Comment on the use of upper and lower case letters. For example, say, "I need a capital letter here because it's someone's name, and names always have a capital letter at the beginning."
- Comment on word spacing. For example, say, "I need to leave a space here because what comes after is a new word."
- Comment on punctuation. For example, say, "I need to add a period because it's the end of the sentence."
- Ask, "Now, what am I missing?" (Depending on the children's developmental levels, the question might be only rhetorical.)
- Implement only a few of these suggestions and keep the writing simple and short. Doing that will let all the children keep focus and attend during the whole Shared Writing experience. When the pieces are complete, the children will be able to read and reread them more independently.

After the Shared Writing, act on any of these suggestions:

- Read the piece aloud carefully to model the proofreading and editing process. You might think aloud, "I have to read this over to check it. That is what good writers do."
- Read the piece as a Shared Reading and invite individuals to have a turn.
- Discuss where the text might be placed in the room.

The Natural Use of Names

Working with children's names affords many opportunities to promote literacy as well as to foster effective classroom management. A child's name is often the first piece of text that he or she learns to recognize and read. "Hey! That's me! That says my name!" All children have a keen interest in themselves, and teachers can use this interest to engage children in the world of writing.

Welcome Sign: On the first day of school, we often put a "Welcome" sign, including all the children's first names, on the door or easel. From the moment they entered, we observed, many children smiled, commented, or pointed at their names. "There's my name!" "There are two Zachs in my class!"

Name Cards: In a Kindergarten classroom, it is often tempting to write the children's names for them to ensure that the work goes home with the appropriate children. Although doing this keeps order and organization in the classroom, it robs the children of an opportunity to write for a significant purpose. Even if the children can print only the first letter of their name, the letter becomes their recognizable mark and an opportunity to teach them to print the remaining letters of their name. Name cards are valuable in this teaching.

Use of Name Cards at Various Centres

1. Be sure to create many class sets of name cards and place them at the various centres in the class, including the Home/Dramatic Play centre. The children may refer to these cards when they are writing receipts or phone messages and need to know how to spell classmates' names.
2. At the Visual Arts centre when children need to print their name, have them do so in the top left-hand corner of the paper before beginning to work. This practice encourages left-to-right progression. Name

---

cards could be hole-punched and attached with a ring to make a book for children to read and refer to when necessary.

3. It can be valuable to place a class set of name cards in the Reading centre, as well. Depending on their developing language skills, the children can read through the names and sort them in different ways:
   - by first letter (All the names begin with the same letter.)
   - by last letter (All the names end with the same letter.)
   - by number of letters (All the names have, for example, seven letters.)
   - by double letters (All the names have, for example, *tt*.)
   - by presence of the same two letters (All the names have, for example, an *a* and an *e*.)
   - by alphabetical order

   While working with the teacher, children can be challenged to describe their sorting results. For example, the names of five children start with the letter *d*; seven children have six letters in their name; no children have names that begin with the letter *q*. It can be valuable to discuss these results orally and then share them in the large group. This activity could be extended by asking the child to use pictures and writing to record information about the sorting experience. The teacher could also take a photograph of the child's sorting to evaluate and assess this learning, as well as to share it with the child's parents.

Taking attendance with name cards

Teachers often take daily attendance by laying out name cards on a table and having the children place them in a basket to indicate their presence. This system works well and provides a literacy opportunity for children to read their own names, as well as the names of classmates. It also provides a chance to notice individual differences between names, for example, initial or final letter, or number of letters.

This learning can be extended by changing the name cards regularly and increasing their level of literacy difficulty throughout the year: at the beginning, the cards could show first names and then be replaced by a set of cards revealing the children's last names. Following that, the cards could present a short and simple, repetitive sentence such as "Jessica is at school today." All the cards would be the same, except for the name, so that the children could still identify their name if the entire sentence was too challenging. For more advanced learners, the full sentence affords the opportunity to read individual words, discuss the need for spaces between words, and identify the punctuation at the end of the sentence.

Over time, maybe once a month, the teacher could make a new set of attendance cards, repeating particular words to help develop sight vocabulary — be sure to use different sentence punctuation to introduce children to periods, exclamation marks, and question marks. Old cards could be bound into a book and added to the Reading centre (see Chapter 4) for children to revisit and consolidate their learning.

Simple sentences such as these make successful attendance cards.
[Name] loves school.
Is [Name] at school today?
[Name] is a student in Room 104.
[Name] is learning about shoes.
(Substitute other classroom learning.)

Using names for classroom management

When children are gathered on the carpet ready for home or lined up for Gym or Library, it is an optimum time to develop listening and auditory discrimination skills as well as phonemic awareness. The teacher might say, "If your name has a *t* in it, please go and line up," and the children would be expected to listen and respond appropriately. Such invitations might include the following literacy challenges:

- identifying the ending letter (e.g., if your name ends with the letter *r*)
- identifying the beginning letter (e.g., if your name begins with the letter *s*)
- counting the number of letters (e.g., if your name has eight letters)
- considering a specific letter or letters (e.g., if your name has a *t* and an *h*)
- determining missing letters (e.g., if your name doesn't have an *n*)

Personal Reading Time

Providing daily reading time is essential. We agree with Frank Smith when he says in *Joining the Literacy Club* that children learn to read by reading. Children need quality time to choose books that interest them, to enjoy their reading, and to practise their skills. In our classrooms, we scheduled a time each day for the children to select and read books of their choice. We insisted that they read independently and not disturb others.

We kept the reading time to 5 to 10 minutes at first, but built it up as the year progressed and as children's attention spans grew longer. By carefully establishing routines, we ensured that everyone would find the time productive.

Teachers can use this personal reading time effectively. We observed the children as they read or retold stories from the pictures or by memory. We noted book choices and encouraged the children to select books that had been read aloud or used for Shared Reading. We also noted the reading skills children used, the intensity of their interest, and their ability to concentrate. Some teachers like to use part of this time to model their interest in reading by reading themselves — we found that by doing this, we had a perfect opportunity to become familiar with new books from the library/resource centre.

At the end of the reading time, children often spontaneously share their enthusiasm for or frustration with a particular book. In this way, the children are exposed to different opinions and preferences. The children like to choose books that their peers recommend. Some teachers have the children keep a record of what they read.

Buddy Reading Program

We recognized that children need many opportunities to read and write and practise their developing literacy skills. We therefore created more opportunities for support in reading and writing activities by pairing our Kindergarten students with older children who were more proficient. Such Buddy Reading activities help to ensure that Cambourne's critical conditions of feedback/response, immersion, and practice are present in the Kindergarten classroom.

Buddy Reading works best, we found, when the older children are not extremely accomplished readers. When their partners are accomplished, the younger children often feel intimidated and then assume an observer's role. If the skill levels of the children are relatively close, then the younger children often feel encouraged to read familiar pattern books or chart-paper texts: this helps them feel positive about their developing skills. We found that twinning older primary students with Kindergarten students worked well.

Since most of the time the older children do the reading, we provided basic training. We used some Shared Reading sessions to demonstrate how to read to a younger child and how to encourage the child to read independently. We stressed that any miscues were not to be treated as mistakes. We suggested that the older readers offer a correction only if the meaning changed — if a child substituted "Grandma" for "Grandmother," we would advise ignoring the miscue.

Talking with both classes about how to select a book is good practice. If some of the "readers" were not proficient, we encouraged the partners to choose simple pattern books, one-word picture books, alphabet books, or familiar rhymes or chants. Younger readers typically chose a familiar book, maybe one of their own making, a pattern book, or a chart-paper text they had helped make. If the children were second language learners, we offered first language material to share. Choice of materials is critical.

Creating conditions that promote success is important. We encouraged the children to decide at the end of each session which material would be shared at the next visit. The designated reader could then take away the material and practise it. At large-group time we encouraged the children to select another book if the reading became too difficult — we did not want to embarrass the more proficient readers or put them in the position of teacher.

Each child has a designated partner. We tried to schedule this activity once a week and required the children to fill in a simple reading log. The partners noted the titles of the books read, wrote comments about the reading materials, and recorded any particular problems they encountered with the reading. They also made requests for new materials.

Date	Readers	Title	Comment
Oct 12 2010	Pashalia KaTIE	The boy in the drawer	we liked the part where she turned on the cold ✓
Oct 26 2010	Katie	I know an old lady	when she swallowed the fly was the best part It sure is funny!

The teacher's check mark and comment "It sure is funny!" reveals that she has reviewed the log kept by a pair of Buddy Readers.

Teaching the older buddies how to make their readings interesting and constructive is important. For a picture book, older buddies need to know how to hold the book so both partners can see it, to talk about the pictures, to predict what might happen next, to use an animated voice, and to point out the title, author's name, and illustrator's name. If the reading selection is a piece of non-fiction, they should be reminded to point out how non-fiction differs from fiction — non-fiction can be read from anywhere in the book, the table of contents helps the reader find the appropriate section, and headings, graphs, and diagrams offer more information. As for the younger buddies, be sure to emphasize the role of a good listener and how to ask questions.

Buddy Reading provides both partners with many authentic reasons to listen, discuss, and read. The audience is always built in, and a coach is always available. The role of coach or audience changes as the situation dictates. Sometimes the older children read, sometimes the younger children read, and often, they share the reading.

Outdoor Play

Outdoor play is a necessary whole-class activity in the Kindergarten schedule. While outside, the children can take part in self-directed, structured, and educational play. They will have many opportunities to develop their large- and small-muscle coordination skills (e.g., running, skipping, jumping, climbing, throwing, and hitting). In addition, they have real reasons to talk, listen, write, read, and plan.

Outdoor play is an opportunity to extend classroom work. To stimulate learning, occasionally bring outside the following items from the classroom:

- books to be read aloud to the large group on a sunny, warm day
- a bucket of books for a private book time or Reading Buddy session
- chalk for drawing and writing on the pavement
- writing materials such as clipboards, cardboard, markers, and crayons
- paints to create individual pictures or co-operative murals
- a sand table along with some props and materials from the indoor Sand centre
- a water table from the Water centre, along with related materials such as wands to blow bubbles or large bottles to fill, measure, and compare

From time to time, you can create an additional, outdoor literacy experience, such as a Car Wash centre.

In the large group, read aloud a book about car washes. Two good ones are *Five Little Monkeys Wash the Car* by Eileen Christelow or *The Scrubbly-Bubbly Car Wash* by Irene O'Garden. Ask the children what they know about car washes and whether they have ever been in one. Still in the large group, discuss all the things in a car wash and ask the children to brainstorm what items would be needed to create a pretend car wash on the playground.

Arrange for plastic ride-on cars to be washed with large sponges and cloths by workers wearing aprons or large rain jackets and using buckets and soapy water. Lanes can be drawn on the pavement to create a route for the cars to drive through. During the Literacy and the Arts activity time, children can work at the Drawing/Writing table to create advertisements and pricing signs for the car wash, which can be taped up on the walls outside during outdoor play. In addition, the children at the car wash can use clipboards and pencils to write out receipts for the customers. A cash register, telephone, and appointment book will further promote literacy.

Buddy Writing

On occasion, our Buddy Readers worked together on a piece of writing. Such writing might include a review of the book or a recommendation for other fiction and non-fiction resources to be purchased. We encouraged both partners to work together to compose, write, record, and illustrate these pieces of writing.

Materials for Outdoor Play

These standard materials can encourage literacy as well as physical development:

- outdoor climbing equipment
- a large sandbox
- sand toys, such as sieves, shovels, and pails
- large models of construction vehicles, such as trucks and diggers
- tricycles, wagons, scooters, hula hoops, and signs
- skipping ropes, Frisbees, beanbags, Styrofoam baseball bats, small plastic hockey sticks, and small soft balls

As for storage, some of the smaller materials such as ropes, beanbags, and balls can be returned to the classroom in a large, net bag or stored in a large garbage pail.

Outdoor Extensions

This pattern of discussion, material gathering, and sign making can be followed and extended to transform a portion of the outdoor playground into

- a gas station
- a drive-thru restaurant
- a drive-in movie theatre

A child has illustrated playing with sticks during outdoor play and provided a caption about it.

At the end of an outdoor play session, the children are always full of stories about what has happened, and many have questions or comments that they are eager to share — "Today, I was able to make it all the way to the top of the climber" or "I went down the slide 13 times and I know because I counted." These are meaningful experiences, and they can often stimulate an interest in picture making and drawing. Teachers can support this interest by challenging some of the children to draw or write about what they made or did while outside. For others it may be more appropriate to orally share their work in the large-group celebration time.

Borrow-a-Book Program

In our Kindergarten classrooms, the borrowing of books was an integral part of our literacy program. We found it helped to establish a concrete link between the home and the school in the important task of learning to read and write. Research shows that children who have been read to before arriving at school have a better chance for later academic success than those children who have not had such experiences. We believe the development of literacy is a shared responsibility, and so we spent time each day helping the children to select reading materials to share with their families.

We collected a wide range of reading materials that represented children of different cultures, physical abilities, races, gender roles, and languages. Some titles we found especially useful are *Amazing Grace* by Mary Hoffman, *Cleversticks* by Bernard Ashley, and *Mama Zooms* by Jane Cowen-Fletcher. We were careful to include materials in different languages, such as a Chinese version of *Where's Spot?* by Eric Hill, so both the children and their families could take part in the reading. Sensitive to home situations, we included wordless picture books for parents who might not be literate, first language materials for those families who could read only in a first language other than English, and materials that represented a variety of topics, cultures, genres, and levels of reading and listening ability. We enlisted our teacher-librarian to help the children borrow during their regularly scheduled Library/Resource time. We regularly borrowed library books for the Borrow-a-Book program and our read-aloud times.

We encouraged the children to borrow reading materials that their family members could read to them. The children also borrowed materials that they could share with their siblings or other family members. We first used these materials for instruction and then through this borrowing, the children were able to practise, reinforce, and demonstrate their learning to their families. Some teachers like to include a record card for the children and their family members to note the name of the book borrowed, the date, and their responses.

We invited the families to comment in either their first language or English, and time was set aside for these comments to be read. This dialogue was very helpful in creating a fuller understanding of the children's interests, attitudes, and skills in the acquisition of literacy.

Several Borrow-a-Book entries with parent and teacher comments follow at the top of page 35.

To emphasize the program's value, consider providing a special bag for carrying these materials home. The bag can be either made of any sturdy material such as waterproof cotton, linen, or burlap or purchased commercially. Label the bag with the school name and class only. We used these bags from one year to the next to save on cost. Other teachers prefer to have the children carry their books home in their knapsacks.

Date	Title	Reader	Comment
Nov 8/2010	Mr. Gumpy's Motor Car	Tomas and Mom	Tomas read parts quite well – difficult words seemed to come easy, little words not so!
Nov 11/2010	Where the Wild Things are	Mom	A strange book but Tomas loved it. MS
Nov 16/2010	Wilfrid Gordon McDonald Partridge	Mom	Tomas loves this book! Lots of "talk"! Could we have one he can read? Absolutely! Tch
Nov 19/2010	Just like Daddy	Tomas and Mom	He did great. We read it several times! Please one for him to read + one for us to read MS. OK tch

This excerpt from a Borrow-a-Book log shows communication between a parent and the teacher.

A teacher's tracking sheet typically shows the first name of each child on the left side, the letters *M T W Th* and *F* repeated four times for four weeks at the bottom, and numerous graph-like squares. As a child borrows a book, such as *Where's Spot?*, the teacher records the title in the appropriate square and checks it off when the book is returned.

It is also important to keep an accurate record of each child's choices. We did so in case the book card went home and got lost; then at least, we had a record of who read what and when. The books that the children borrowed from the library/resource centre had their own computer-generated record that we found useful in helping to track down overdue titles.

It is important to discuss the Borrow-a-Book program with parents/guardians. For a Parent Night or Curriculum Night, plan to outline your expectations for their involvement. You might also like to send home a letter outlining how parents and caregivers can support their children when reading at home.

Dear Parents/Guardians,

Re: Borrow-a-Book Program

Learning to read is a significant part of a child's academic development, and parents play an important role in this accomplishment. Many parents read to their children nightly, sharing books from their home collections, as well as books from the local library. This practice is a wonderful way for children to develop an interest in reading.

With this letter we are introducing a way for you to extend your involvement in your child's reading — the Kindergarten Borrow-a-Book program. Borrow-a-Book is a daily program in which children independently select books from an appropriate classroom collection and take them home to share with family and friends. Some of the books will be simple picture books or pattern books appropriate for the child to read to you; other books are best suited for parents to read to children. Since these books come from school, the children feel ownership and a sense of responsibility for them.

Set aside a special time and place to read these Borrow-a-Books. Sometimes this undivided time together can be just as significant as the book. While reading, talk to your child about the book by addressing some of the following ideas.

1. Read the title and the name of the author or illustrator, and help the child make connections. ("This is the same author who wrote the book that we read last week.")

2. Examine the cover together and make predictions about content. ("There is a family on the cover and they have a picnic basket and a tent. I wonder if they are going camping.")

3. Talk about favorite parts and characters. ("I like the part when the dog jumped up on the counter and ate all the cookies — that was funny.")

4. Make connections to the text. ("It reminds me of . . .")

Watch for your first Borrow-a-Book to come home on Monday. It will be in a Ziploc bag and accompanied by a log for you and your child to record the date and book read. Welcome to the Kindergarten Borrow-a-Book program! Taking part in it will help enrich your child's reading at home and promote within your child a love of books.

Sincerely,

This program takes considerable time and organization, but the benefits justify the extra effort. We found that the children were eager to read, and the parents appreciated the help the school offered in providing books and in making home reading more manageable. This program also helped parents understand more about the process of learning to read and the critical nature of their role.

Celebrations and Special Events

In addition to the literacy experiences just outlined and the presence of permanent centres, we also promote the potential of celebrations and special events to enrich the literacy activities in the classroom. Teachers can capitalize on celebrations, using them to introduce and develop a variety of skills, knowledge, and attitudes. Celebrations provide an exciting and motivating vehicle for children to acquire language and literacy skills.

A special centre

A table can become the core of a Celebration and Special Event centre, a small, temporary centre. Teachers may set up this table in response to a holiday or a special event such as Chinese New Year or first snowfall. Like other centres, the Celebration and Special Event centre allows teachers to plan in an integrated way. Many of the activities involve speaking, listening, viewing, reading, writing, numeracy, patterning, measuring, dramatizing, singing, playing instruments, drawing, painting, creating, building, observing, exploring, testing hypotheses, and drawing conclusions. Our goal with a Celebration table was to build on some of the children's prior knowledge and introduce others to new cultural experiences and customs, such as Hanukkah and Divali.

We were careful to resist introducing this small centre through contrived whole-class themes, such as winter or apples.

Since these celebrations or events are closely related to the current expressed interests of the children, each manifestation of the centre is different in a number of ways. Celebration and Special Event centres vary in duration, either lasting several days or several weeks. They also vary in nature. They can include collections of real objects, props, models, related books, puzzles, and posters. In the Kindergarten years, the competencies of the children are diverse; hence, the centres vary in intensity and scope. They depend on how many children are interested. We always encouraged the children to pursue their own interests or inquiries.

Providing a wide range of materials that support children at a variety of developmental levels is important. For example, at a centre celebrating Chinese New Year our materials and setup have included the following:

- *concrete/real objects items*, such as gold coins, red envelopes for money, a dragon mask, chopsticks, a wok, and fortune cookies
- *semi-abstract materials*, such as pictures of the dragon parade, posters of the Chinese alphabet, and models of small dragons
- *abstract materials*, such as books that are bias free and avoid stereotypic images and gender roles (e.g., *Ching Chiang and the Dragon's Dance* by Ian Wallace and *Sam and the Lucky Money* by Karen Chinn, illustrated by Cornelius Van Wright and Ying-Hwa Hu)
- a small table or desk
- a bulletin board or easel to display photographs, pictures, posters, and children's work
- writing and drawing materials (e.g., pencils, markers, and graph paper)

Snow! — Capitalizing on Children's Interests

Sometimes, a spontaneous event such as a sudden snowstorm excited and engaged all the children we taught. We capitalized on their interest and, in this instance, created a snow table.

At the outdoor play period we let children play in the snow and then provided them with snow shovels. We invited them to fill up pails with snow and bring it inside to the Water centre. The children then made predictions and estimated how long it would take for the snow to melt. We recorded these predictions with a repetitive pattern:

> Omar thinks it will melt by story time.
> Mei Ling thinks it will melt after activity time.

Depending on their interest, we might add shovels and moulds for the children to create a snowscape or provide other materials, such as sticks, stones, and Playmobil people, to extend their dramatic play and talk.

We fostered thinking about snow-related activities. We sent a letter home to ask the parents to help their children collect objects related to snow, such as skates. We took pictures of the children playing in the snow and invited them to bring in any photographs that showed their family having fun in the snow. We collected models such as snowball ornaments. All of these items came to be featured on the snow table.

We turned the children's attention to books about snow. We read Jack Prelutsky's *It's Snowing! It's Snowing!*, a book of winter poems. We asked the children to go to the library/resource centre and borrow other books about snow, both fiction and non-fiction. Some children offered to illustrate their ideas in a class booklet or made their own snowman-shaped booklet at the Drawing/Writing centre.

We also introduced the game Bingo at this centre, using words generated by the children (e.g., *mittens, hat, snowsuit, earmuffs, boots*). (See Appendix B: Games.) Children gained a good opportunity to learn more vocabulary related to snow.

By listening to the children and observing them carefully as they play, teachers can determine the interests of the children and offer many more literacy experiences that are meaningful to them. Chinese New Year and snow are just two celebrations and special events that may excite the children and stimulate their interest in literacy activities.

3 The Drawing/Writing Centre

Although we recommend strategically placing writing materials at all centres in the Kindergarten, the Drawing/Writing centre is the primary place where children are regularly invited but never pressured to draw and write. This invitational approach is an alternative to the practice of some of our colleagues of providing a specific time where everyone is expected to complete a drawing or writing task.

An Invitation to Write

We observed that when given choice, children even at the scribble stage show interest in and gravitate towards writing activities. More sophisticated writers serve as role models and naturally motivate others. We recognized that even before coming to school many children use conventional print, make marks, and create pictures. Regardless of economic and social background, almost all the children have some exposure to print. Most children recognize various symbols and signs in the environment — for example, Home Depot, Crosswalk, School — and they are eager to make their own marks. Creating a Drawing/Writing centre honors this interest.

Drawing and writing seem to flourish in an atmosphere where children are expected but not pressured to write in one form or another. At this centre, many informal discussions take place, and the more developed writers willingly and naturally answer the queries of the beginning writers. For example: "How does *water* start?" "It starts like the picture of a whale on your alphabet chart. Here, see."

Our Drawing/Writing centre was successful for several reasons. The routines were well established, and the materials were shared and stored in labelled bins and baskets. We ensured that the children had real purposes and meaningful reasons to write as opposed to simply copying or filling in the blanks. We introduced them to various formats, including lists, stories, directions, letters, and signs. For example, the children made their own signs for their work in the Sand centre or in the Home/Dramatic Play centre. Although paper, writing materials, clipboards, and whiteboards were always available for use at other centres, some children might prefer to do this work at the Drawing/Writing centre.

Children write for real reasons related to their play at other centres.

LEVHR

Leave here.

pzzA 4 SAL

Pizza for sale.

All pieces of writing, regardless of surface form, were accepted and encouraged.

The children became knowledgeable about the wide range of competency on the drawing/writing continua. They were often heard to say, "I used to use all capitals like you do. Now I use some small letters." Hearing such comments reassured the beginning writers about their own efforts. It also reinforced their understanding about the continuous nature of learning. When identifying the progress of others, the more sophisticated writers gained additional practice, confidence, and pride in their own writing skills. They saw the progress they had made.

Our experience with young writers taught us the importance of children selecting their own topics and reasons to write. That is why we have a designated Drawing/Writing centre as well as writing materials available for the children to use at all of the centres in the room. During the play at various classroom centres, the children had real reasons to write, talk, and listen. This ownership of writing fostered the children's interest and promoted true engagement with learning. We assured all our students that they had many interesting ideas to express through drawing and words, many stories to tell, and purposes for doing so. The children accepted this challenge, and their drawing and writing improved.

We provided invitations to write from the very first day at school. At the Drawing/Writing centre we accepted all efforts from scribble to sentences and scaffolded the children as they progressed through different developmental stages. The Drawing/Writing centre was one of the first learning centres to be introduced.

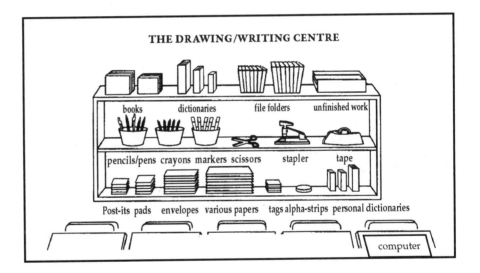

A well-stocked Drawing/Writing centre serves as the classroom hub for writing activities, but children will also find natural opportunities to write at other centres.

Developing Writing Skills Early

At the beginning of our careers, we used to write *for* the children, accepting their dictations and believing that they were too young to write for themselves. We even wrote the children's names for them. They often copied our work, inserting a few words they had memorized, perhaps *mommy* or *daddy*. However, as we reflected on our practice, we came to realize that the children were not taking part in the real process of writing. We were doing most of the thinking and problem solving. As a result, even at the beginning of the year with the youngest of the children, we began to ask them to try to write for themselves.

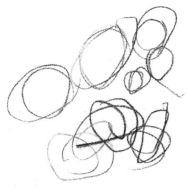

Corby

Jack

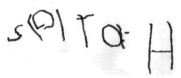

Sarah

Charlie

Within one classroom, children's ability will range from making fairly random shapes as Corby did to representing all the letters in a name and using a mix of upper and lower case letters as Charlie did.

"All the people are cheering for goals." Here is an example of where it would be appropriate to teach the child about putting spaces between words.

We subsequently helped the children to write their own names by providing name cards in both capital and lower case letters for the children to use as a reference. We accepted the approximations of these names. Some children represented their names only with a mark, others copied some of the letters, and still others wrote their whole names independently. Four representative samples appear at left. We expected a wide range of performances dependent upon their previous writing experiences — scribbles, dots, dashes to mimic text, letter attempts, single letters, clusters of letters, and recognizable words. (See "Mileposts to Help Guide Teacher Observations of Children Drawing and Writing," pages 49 to 54.) Formal and informal conferences helped the children make progress in their writing.

Initially, we helped the children form the letters, see sound–symbol relationships, and determine the context in which the word they were working on appeared in the whole sentence. As we observed a need for instruction, we either offered specific teaching to the one child or incorporated that learning into a Shared Writing time. For example, we might notice the common problem of children stringing all their letters together, without a letter space between each word, or separating the words with a dot or dash. Where appropriate we showed the children how to separate the words in a sentence using a finger.

Turning to the computer

We also encouraged the children to use the computer to communicate and to share their knowledge. We resisted the temptation to use the computer only for games, preferring to let the children use it as a tool for a multitude of communication purposes. Some children used the computer as others used a pencil to make signs, write notes, and compose stories.

We found that the children came to school with varying degrees of experience with computers. A few children were computer literate, knowing how to operate the keyboard. Some had experience playing with games; many had seen only adults using computers while others had no experience whatsoever. Acknowledging a range of competencies, we realized that many computer tutors were readily available. The more experienced computer users helped the beginners to become more proficient. Unlike adults who often balk when introduced to a computer, the children had little or no fear or hesitancy in approaching it.

In the computer lab and the classroom, we liked to pair the children so they could support each other. Grouping the children in this way ensured that the use of the computer was socially interactive instead of isolating. The computer in the classroom was used throughout the day. When the class went to the computer lab, usually with a teacher delivering preparation time, we encouraged the children to work with other communication programs, such as *WiggleWorks* or *A to Z Reading* (www.atozreading.com), which have both reading and writing components.

Materials That Encourage Children to Draw and Write

Since writing and reading are inextricably linked, we liked to use a book to introduce the children to the excitement of these pursuits. A marvellous book for this purpose is *More Than Anything Else* by Marie Bradby (illustrated by Chris Soentpiet). The book chronicles the story of a boy who desperately wants to learn to read and write. Such a resource helps youngsters understand the value of literacy learning and can stimulate a class discussion about why reading and writing are important. Children can begin to realize that people read for pleasure and for information, and write to share ideas and communicate.

The drawing and writing book

During the first few days of school, children who chose to write during the Literacy and the Arts period each received a book of blank paper. We invited them to use these books for drawing or writing. We also asked them to decorate the front of their personal drawing and writing book and to include their name.

Children unable to write their names were encouraged to make a mark that they would later recognize or print the first letter of their name. We were always available to demonstrate letter formation, perhaps showing it in the air or on a piece of paper. We resisted writing children's names because we wanted to give the message that we expected the children to write for themselves.

During large Gathering Times we scheduled an opportunity for the children to share their drawings and writings and gain feedback. We also encouraged the group to respond positively, perhaps saying, "It's impressive you labelled all the parts of the giraffe that you drew." We commented on the unique features of each child's writing and drawing and modelled how to ask questions: "I see that you have . . .," "How did you make . . .?"

Drawing/Writing centre resources

The Drawing/Writing centre we established was always filled with inviting materials to encourage children to write for a variety of purposes. Below is a checklist of recommended resources:

- paper of many sizes, shapes, colors, and weights
- strips of paper for captions for paintings and drawings
- pencils, crayons, and markers of many thicknesses and colors
- small chalkboards and white boards
- a computer

- rulers, date stamps
- motivational materials, such as blank Post-it notes, tags, envelopes, notepads, labels, cards, calendars, postcards, and message pads — materials that the children see adult writers using every day
- scissors, glue sticks, tape, staplers, paper clips
- other materials specific to writing, including alphabet boards and picture dictionaries
- alphabet cards and alphabet books
- two personal writing folders for each child, one for finished work and one for work in progress
- hanging file folders to hold the work-in-progress folders
- books about writing (e.g., *Dear Bunny: A Bunny Love Story* by Michaela Morgan, illustrated by Caroline Jayne Church)

Appropriate materials for all centres

Children, naturally inquisitive, are interested in making and then in sharing their new discoveries. It is critical to capitalize on their interest by making writing materials available at *all* centres in the classroom. For example, leave notepads, Post-its, and pencils in the Home/Dramatic Play centre, whiteboards at the Water centre, and chalkboards and clipboards at the Sand centre. Ensure too that strips of paper and markers are available at the Visual Arts centre so that the children can add writing to their paintings. Nonetheless, the Drawing/Writing centre remains the main centre where drawing or writing is the primary purpose.

Literacy Activities in the Drawing/Writing Centre

In addition to providing materials related to writing at the Drawing/Writing centre, many special activities can be introduced at the Drawing/Writing centre to stimulate the development of early writing skills. The following open-ended activities have proven to be successful with a wide range of learners. They provide opportunities for children to recognize and form the letters of the alphabet, develop sound–symbol relationships, and distinguish upper and lower case letters, all without the use of restrictive worksheets. Our goal was always to help the children discover a love of drawing, writing, and communicating.

Focusing first on names

Chapter 2 presents a number of general ways in which teachers can capitalize on children's interest in and familiarity with their names. In the section "The Natural Use of Names" we outline how use of names can promote classroom management, the keeping of attendance, and centre play.

Here a few ways of learning the names of other students and using names to promote discussion.

Name Templates: Children can do this activity on the floor or on a table at the centre. Have the children spell out their names with plastic letters and then trace the outline of the letters onto a piece or a strip of cardboard. Children can use these templates and magnetic letters to reassemble and spell their name. Use a book ring to keep all the children's name templates in one place. Doing so will help enable the children to spell out the names of their classmates, as well as their own names.

Once children no longer need the signs, notes, and so forth they created for play at other centres, remember to ensure that the pieces are stored in their finished work folders.

Organizing plastic alphabet letters can be challenging. One way is to sort the letters into a fishing tackle box or a sewing box where there are many divided sections. Each section could be labelled with the appropriate letter so that the children can easily tidy up the materials. When letters are loose in a bin or basket, it can be difficult for children to find the appropriate letter; the sorting system helps children to discriminate between similar letters, such as *b*, *d*, and *p*.

Books about Names: There are many wonderful published books, both fiction and non-fiction, about people's names and where they come from. During a large-group read-aloud session, read some of the following books, and share a discussion about why names are important.

- *Chrysanthemum* by Kevin Henkes
- *Mommy Doesn't Know My Name* by Suzanne Williams
- *Andy: That's My Name* by Tomie dePaola
- *My Name Is Yoon* by Helen Recorvits

Have the children conduct some research at home. Tell them to ask their family why they have the name they do and where it came from. Upon next return to school, each child can share the information orally with the class or take part in a pair-share activity. During a pair-share two children talk about their experiences in turn and then share their thoughts with the large group.

The book *Mommy Doesn't Know My Name* by Suzanne Williams can lead beautifully into a discussion about nicknames and why we have them. Invite the children to share their personal nicknames and use these names and those in the book to brainstorm a long list of nicknames, for example, Toots, Nate, Pumpkin, Honeybun, Skipper, Junior, Buddy, Peanut, and Sweetie. Some names might even be similar and could lead into a graphing activity.

Using personal drawing and writing books

In an effort to teach children to write and form letters, Kindergarten programs often present worksheets that ask children to repeatedly form a letter and then circle the illustrations that begin with that letter. While this exercise helps children practise letter formation and sound–symbol relationship, there are other more effective and meaningful ways to help children develop the same letter formation skills as well as other appropriate writing skills.

It is more challenging, interesting, and meaningful to provide each child with a personal drawing and writing book. Our book design was to have 10 blank pieces of 8 1/2 inch by 11 inch white paper, stapled at the left, with a construction paper cover. Use the same color of construction paper for all the children's books so that these books can be easily identified in the classroom. Plan to store the books in a labelled bin for identification and storage. It is important for children to be able to gain independent access to their books when they are ready to draw or write at the Drawing/Writing centre during the Literacy and the Arts activity period. They thereby have an opportunity to read and distinguish their books from the others in the class.

The children can label the cover of the writing book with their names and the title "My Drawing and Writing Book." Some children may be able to write this title independently by referencing a card or an easel where it is written. All children should be encouraged to write their own name. The placement of a set of name cards at the Drawing/Writing centre will provide assistance.

The children need to have regular opportunities to write and draw in this book. Allowing them to select their own topics will increase their commitment and interest in their work. For example, a. child who loves to watch cartoons may want to write about a favorite episode, while a Kindergartener who has just become a big sister may want to draw and write about the big news.

Encourage the children to begin with an illustration. When they proudly approach you with a finished product, respond by saying, "Wow! Tell me about your picture." Be careful not to make a judgment about the picture. Sometimes the picture looks like a cow to an adult, but it is really a horse. Inaccurately labelling a picture will likely discourage a young child, so, we find, it is always best to let the child provide the explanation. Saying "Tell me about your work" makes that possible.

Once the children have orally shared a story to accompany their picture, they can be encouraged to write it down. If the picture is of a race car, simply say the word slowly and ask the child, "What letters do you hear?" Encourage the child to record all the letters that he or she hears. The results will vary with the range of auditory discrimination skills within the class. Some beginning writers might record only an *r* or *rc*. More advanced writers might record *ras cr* or even simple sentences like the one shown below.

These individual teacher conferences need to be tailored to the needs of the particular child. As an example, you might take this teaching time to show the child where to use a period or write a letter of the alphabet in the writing book and encourage the child to try a few extra for practice.

"This is a race car on a track." The child who wrote the text within this picture has a good understanding of sound–letter relationships and word spacing.

In addition, if looking at the child's caption above, print the conventional words *race car* and ask the child to compare his or her spelling of the words to the "way they look in the book." Doing this gives the child a chance to notice differences and learn to spell new words: "Your words have an *s* and a *c* and my words have two *c*'s." It is important to refer to a word's correct spelling as "the way it looks in a book," as opposed to "right" or "wrong." This subtle distinction allows young writers to maintain confidence in their skills and continue to take risks and develop new understandings.

Once the children have completed their drawings and writing, it can be very powerful for the teacher to write a note in response to this hard work. This note should be written on the opposite page so as not to impose on the children's efforts. It should be written in clear primary printing, with proper letter format, to ensure that the children can identify the letters and learn to model their attempts on the text. A note might read as follows.

Dear Grace,

I love your picture and writing. You did a super job.

From,

Mrs. Flemington

Many children will initially need the letter read to them. In time, however, they will be able to identify their own name, as well as other repeated words, such as *dear*, *love*, and *picture*. Challenge the children to locate and circle particular words. You might also omit the children's names and ask them to fill in the blank space.

For more advanced language learners, the teacher may want to leave many blanks to be completed. The children can thereby build on previous models and a bank of written and sight vocabulary. The outline below provides an example.

Dear _____,

I _____ your picture and writing. _____ did a _____ job.

From,

_____

Writing a positive response in the form of a letter provides an opportunity to discuss this writing format with more advanced literacy learners. In an individual conference, the teacher could point out how the letter begins with *Dear*, has two special places for a comma, and gets into its substance below the person's name. The teacher could also talk about how a letter is different from the text in a list or a story. For example, a letter follows a special format, a list helps to record information and appears in a column, and a story features characters and a setting, and has a beginning, a middle, and an end.

Clearly, it would not be possible to meet and have these individual literacy conferences with every child, every day, but these short and meaningful meetings can take place several times per week. In time, children will become more familiar with the process, and they will develop more language skills and be able to do more of the writing independently. Be sure to invite the children to share their work with the class during large-group times. This sharing will help develop confidence and inspiration for the next writing experience.

Writing personal stories

With all the meaningful writing experiences in the classroom, the children will begin to see themselves as successful writers, and the more advanced language learners will begin to write pieces with more words and sentences. Over the course of a few days, a child might write and draw several related pieces, such as these:

I lk t p w mi crs (I like to play with my cars.)

I lk t p w mi ts (I like to play with my tea set.)

I lk t p w mi stfd a (I like to play with my stuffed animals.)

With construction paper and book coils or staples, these personal pieces can be easily assembled into a book. The child might be introduced to the computer to type the text which could be printed out with space for illustrations. This text could also be keyed in by a classroom volunteer or junior student. Over time, the child could be taught to include other features in the publication:

- title page (title and author name)
- dedication
- publication information (date, school name and address)
- author information (as simple as a school photograph, as detailed as a child-written text)
- Comments page (place for readers to write comments about the book)
- list of other books published by the same author

Writing class books using a pattern book as a model

Class books can be simple and include little text or can be more elaborate and include a great deal, but it is always effective to begin with a commercially published book as a model. At the beginning of the year, the classic book and song *Mary Wore Her Red Dress* (Merle Peek) is a terrific choice for reading aloud at a Gathering Time. To complement the reading, you might take individual photographs of the children on the first day and alter the text appropriately.

Original song text: First verse	*Altered text*
Mary wore her red dress,	Amid wore his white shirt,
Red dress,	White shirt,
Red dress,	White shirt,
Mary wore her red dress,	Amid wore his white shirt,
All day long!	All day long!

Once all the students have heard the story at Gathering Time, then children at the Drawing/Writing centre can bring the project to fruition. Photographs and accompanying texts can be placed in a photo album to create a class book. Ensure that the text appears in large clear font or have it easily typed on the computer. The layout for each page should be the same so that the children can use the location of the text on the page to help read it.

You might also work with a classic book such as *Brown Bear, Brown Bear, What Do You See?* by Bill Martin Jr. Read the book to the class and then with interested students at the Drawing/Writing centre, use the text to create a book modelled on the picture book's format. The children could each draw self-portraits, and the text could read something like this:

"Jasmine, Jasmine, who do you see?"

"I see Marcus looking at me."

"Marcus, Marcus, who do you see?"

"I see Omar looking at me."

"Omar, Omar . . ."

This class book could also be created with photographs. Each page can be easily tailored to the needs of the children. Some children will write their own

Although the original picture book has a strong rhythm, in the class book it is much less important to achieve this. The main thing is that the children see their names in the story and can follow the story pattern.

names while the teacher writes the rest of the text. More advanced literacy learners might be able to write the entire page of text.

When selecting books that provide a springboard to assist children in creating their own versions, we always looked for materials with limited text, a strong pattern or rhyme, and a good picture–text relationship. These features help beginning readers unlock print as they help readers make accurate guesses about the print.

Pattern books that make good springboards for individual or class books include these:

- *I Went Walking* by Sue Williams
- *Time for Bed* by Mem Fox
- *I Like Books* by Anthony Browne
- *Five Little Monkeys Jumping on a Bed* by Eileen Christelou
- *The Doorbell Rang* by Pat Hutchison
- *Eating the Alphabet Fruits and Vegetables from A to Z* by Lois Ehlert
- *Polar Bear, Polar Bear, What Do You Hear?* by Bill Martin Jr. and Eric Carle
- *The House That Jack Built* by Diana Mayo
- *The Little Red Hen* by Paul Galdone

Beyond the patterning, read-alouds allow the teacher to point out significant text features, including title page, dedication, date and place of publication, and author information. The teacher might reinforce this teaching about specific book features and their importance by including them in published class books. She could involve children in voting on the book title and determining the dedication. In a class book, the teacher might also include a list of other books published by the class and a "Comments page" for adult readers to record comments about the book. In addition, a copyright symbol (©) could be introduced and added to the inside cover.

Writing in different formats

Among the carefully selected books that are read aloud during group time and later added to the Reading centre are titles of many different shapes, sizes, and formats. All of these formats provide meaningful models for children to create their own books at the Drawing/Writing centre.

Lift-the-Flap Books: The books of Lucy Cousins, Eric Hill, and Harriet Ziefert provide great models, and the children can make individual or group question-and-answer books or riddle books. Here is a riddle: "What is white and fluffy and has two long ears?" The reader could then lift a flap to find an illustration or a photograph of a bunny. The children are free to consult other sources for riddles.

Accordion Books: Take an 8 1/2 by 14 inch piece of legal-sized paper or oversized painting paper, hold it so that the greatest length is horizontal, and fold the paper in half; then, fold the top half back towards the crease and the bottom half back towards the crease so the paper looks like an accordion. This style makes distinct individual sections for separate illustrations. It works well to make a book about things that are red or that come in pairs.

Shape Books: Children can be stimulated to write when a model is shared in a new and interesting way. Use construction paper as a cover, place five or six pages inside, and staple them to make a book in a particular shape. A heart-shaped book can challenge the children to write and draw about things that they love, while a book shaped like a circle can stimulate children to draw and label things in the world that are round.

One way to help children make individual and class repetitive-pattern books is to provide a stem such as "I love . . ." and invite the children to fill in the rest. See the page sample below.

A child has used both a shape — a heart — and a pattern "i lov . . ." to write about mother, hearts, family, and school.

Alphabet Books: There are many wonderful alphabet books and Flora McDonnell's *ABC* is a favorite. Other favorite alphabet books include these:

- *K Is for Kiss Goodnight* by Jill Sardegna
- *Chicka Chicka Boom Boom* by Bill Martin Jr. and John Archambault (illustrated by Lois Ehlert)
- *The Handmade Alphabet* by Laura Rankin
- *M Is for Maple: A Canadian Alphabet* by Michael Ulmer
- *Goodnight Moon ABC Board Book: An Alphabet Book* by Margaret Wise Brown (illustrated by Clement Hurd)
- *Alphabet Rescue* by Audrey Wood (illustrated by Bruce Wood)
- *Kipper's A to Z: An Alphabet Adventure* by Mick Inkpen
- *Alpha Bugs: A Pop-up Alphabet Book* by David A. Carter

The children can create their own mini-alphabet books or you can take a large piece of painting paper and divide it into 26 spaces — this format could be laminated to create a poster or placemat. Invite the children to think of words that begin with each letter, and then draw and write them or even cut out images from a magazine.

Mini Word-Books: During the many large-group Shared Writing experiences you will probably have had, several large word charts would have been created. Post these charts in appropriate places around the classroom. Since it can be difficult to find enough spaces that are at the children's eye level, take down a chart once it has been viewed by all the children, and transform it into a mini word-book. Print each word on a card, and have a group of children illustrate some of the cards; then, use a ring to hold the cards together to form a spiral book. These ringed books can all be placed in a basket at the Drawing/Writing centre so that children can refer to them while they write.

Creating an Environment for Success in the Drawing/Writing Centre

The following section is presented in terms of questions that the reflective practitioner is encouraged to ask about the classroom's Drawing/Writing centre. The answers reflect what we have found to be best practices.

1. How do I efficiently and accurately track the children's progress?

Here is how one effective system might operate:

- Provide each child with one file folder for work in progress.
- Store this work in easily accessible, hanging file folders.
- Store all finished work in file folders that can be kept in your filing cabinet.
- Remember to add writing from the other centres.
- Avoid an overload of paper by regularly culling finished work, keeping some for reporting to parents and sending the rest home.
- Ask the children to date-stamp all work.
- Briefly record, in their writing folders, the results of all conversations about particular skills or knowledge, for example, "Liam is beginning to use more than one letter for a word."

- Have the children who feel comfortable with the writing process record the titles of their stories and their future plans on the inside cover of their unfinished work folder.
- Keep significant pieces of work in the children's individual cumulative portfolios and pass them on to the next year's teacher.

2. How do I ensure that the children are challenged, but not pressured?

- Expose the children to a rich variety of authors and their writing styles.
- Introduce the children to interesting techniques of print and illustrations, for example, the letter format in *A Chair for Baby Bear* by Kaye Umansky or the transparencies in Eric Carle's *Mister Seahorse*.
- Schedule small groups of children for authentic Shared Writing experiences, for example, making menus for the pizza restaurant or a shopping list for the store or a recipe for cookies the class wants to bake.
- Occasionally, pair strong writers with beginning writers (e.g., for brainstorming what a construction worker might have in a toolbox).
- Occasionally, pair strong writers with strong illustrators.
- Schedule time for the children to share their work.
- Focus on what the children can do, what they have learned, and what they need to learn next, in order to tailor your teaching, so it is relevant to the children.
- Treat all mistakes not as mistakes, but as valid attempts and opportunities to learn.
- Focus on only a few teaching points at any one time, so as not to overwhelm and discourage the children. For example, talk about where to begin on a page or the need to put spaces between words.
- Spend equal time with all the children, so they can see that you value all the learning, whether it be first-time scribbles or conventional print.
- Schedule a manageable number of children to interact with each day, balancing time spent circulating at all the centres with time spent conferencing at the Drawing/Writing centre.

3. How can I help parents support their children's efforts to write?

- Share the children's progress regularly, highlighting mileposts.
- Share with parents the consequences of overcorrecting children's attempts at conventional print. Explain that overcorrection erodes self-confidence and the willingness to take risks; it often inhibits the children's writing as the children limit themselves to the words they know and not to their ideas.

Mileposts to Help Guide Teacher Observations of Children Drawing and Writing

For the purposes of observation, we have divided the mileposts into two separate continua: Drawing and Writing. However, in the beginning stages, children do not differentiate between these two processes. They naturally make marks to communicate their ideas and as they make a mark on a paper for the first time, they intuitively see themselves as communicators and writers. Then, as they gain control of their small muscles, develop eye-hand coordination skills, gain experience with the media and print in their environment, see others writing and are invited to write as well, they begin to separate the drawing and writing processes.

To continue to see themselves as writers, they must be invited and expected to write, must see other people write, and must have their efforts accepted and valued.

The developmental mileposts outlined are guidelines only — they are not intended to be all-inclusive or prescriptive. We used them for observation and assessment and to guide our individual and small-group instruction in the Kindergarten classroom.

How children show an interest in drawing and writing

The most obvious ways that children show an interest are by choosing the Drawing/Writing centre and also by drawing and writing at the other centres. They may choose the computer as their writing tool. Once they have written something, they may share their work with a friend or teacher when asked or do so spontaneously. They may even ask to share their work at large-group time or in the library or other classes. Other indications of interest include writing about or drawing several pictures on the same topic or working on a drawing or piece of writing for more than one work period.

How children use drawing materials for drawing

- Children first experiment with one color or two, making marks that may hold changing meaning for them, but are unrecognizable to adults.
- They later use or experiment with more than one color and tool.
- Children begin to join marks into curved and straight lines using one or several colors.
- They make curved lines into circles and ovals, sometimes filling in shapes.
- Taking circles and ovals and lines, they begin to make symbols (e.g., the sun, letters, and numerals).

- Children take circles and lines and begin to make symbols of body images.

- They draw more lines and dots to show a more detailed person, with fingers, feet, clothes, and hair.

- Children make symbols of houses or apartments to enclose people — be sure to observe the chimney position (vertical or horizontal). Some teachers have noted a correlation between the chimney position and the emergent writer: when the chimney is represented in a perpendicular form, children can generally use some forms of conventional print.

- Children add recognizable symbols of other familiar objects in the environment such as trees and flowers.
- They add more details to their illustrations (e.g, earrings on girls, stripes on a boy's shirt).

- Children use a variety of materials and techniques to create different moods or impressions, for example, chalk or oil pastels to indicate snow or black marker outlining so a shape will stand out.
- Children make pictures that have a base line and a sky line.
- They create pictures that have a recognizable story.

- Children begin to use different illustrative techniques such as cartoons, flaps, and borders.
- They make pictures that show profiles, relative sizes, and perspectives.

How children use materials for writing

- Children grip writing tools in a variety of ways. They may use a fist or fingers and thumb.
- They make marks that imitate text in English or other first languages.
- Children use circles and lines to tell stories.

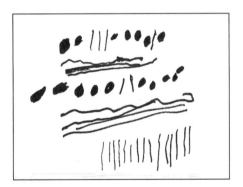

- Children attempt to make letters, usually capitals from their own name.

- Children print random letters in a scattered fashion over their picture or blank paper, often using their own name.
- They later print random letters in a more organized form, for example, vertical or horizontal.
- Children print random letters that imitate text; that is, the text goes from left to right.

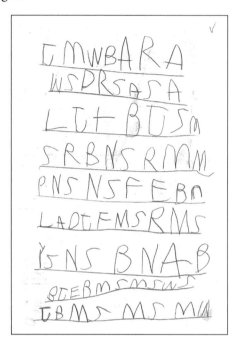

- Children begin to match sounds and symbols by labelling details in their pictures. They often use the strongest letter in the word (e.g., *S* for sun).
- They subsequently use more than one sound for a word, usually strong consonants such as *s*, *c*, and *t*, and long vowels.

- Children come to use more letters of the alphabet accurately.
- They use spaces or dots or lines to show the difference between a word and a letter.

- Children add captions to their pictures.

A child has added a caption meaning Jack-o-Lantern.

- Children use both capital and lower case letters.
- They incorporate some familiar sight words (e.g., *mom* or a friend's name).

A child has included the words Mom *and* Dad *and tried to write* love.

- Children incorporate some repetitive function words such as *the* and *is* into their writing.
- Eventually, they use more accurate spellings.

The child has written "This is a cat and a ghost trying to get the candy but we pulled it back."

While writing occurs at a variety of centres in the classroom, the Drawing/ Writing centre is the hub of literacy development and a place where children regularly draw and write. This centre provides opportunities for children to express their feelings and ideas and produce pieces of work that build on the models found in the books around the classroom.

4

The Reading Centre

In order for children to value and enjoy reading, we, as teachers, must demonstrate our enthusiasm and excitement about books and other reading materials.

As part of this, in our Kindergarten classrooms, we created a large space for celebrating books and reading materials, building excitement about them, and creating the conditions that support the development of literacy. The mere presence of books throughout the room does not automatically invite children into print, however. We recommend carefully selecting a wide range of reading materials to ensure that some will appeal to children of different cultures, reading experiences, developmental levels, and interests. The space in which many of these materials are located is the Reading centre.

In this centre dedicated to reading, children are immersed in a collection of reading materials which allow them to select titles that interest them and that suit their reading ability level. When there are many choices to make, children readily take ownership of their choices.

The non-judgmental and safe atmosphere permits children to flourish as readers. Teachers and other readers give meaningful demonstrations, offer positive feedback, and provide relevant opportunities for beginning readers to practise. As the children interact with their teacher, volunteers, and classmates, they naturally begin to imitate the reading behaviors of more proficient readers — remember that the children will have a range of reading experiences and skills, with some already quite capable, others getting the meaning of a story from the illustrations, and still others lacking much or any experience with books or print.

Promoting a Love of Reading

For children to develop a positive attitude about reading and to read for a variety of purposes, we need to select materials with care. It is essential to include a wealth of reading materials of the highest quality, for example, texts by award-winning authors and illustrators such as Eric Carle, Sheree Fitch, and Bill Martin Jr. If all the children are to find materials relevant to them, we need to ensure that these materials are bias free and representative of many different races, cultures, and linguistic groups. To address the wide range of developmental levels found in the classroom, it is necessary to provide a range of text types including wordless books, pattern books, picture books, stories, non-fiction texts, poetry, and magazines (see "Favorite Books of Different Kinds" on pages 57 to 58).

Books about reading

At the beginning of the year, we suggest, use a book about reading to introduce the Reading centre. A favorite that depicts a child reading or learning to love reading can help youngsters see themselves as successful readers. David McPhail's *Fix-It* is a good example. Throughout the year continue to read books about reading and the process of learning to read. The following titles proved to be most effective for us:

- *I Like Books* by Anthony Browne
- *Reading Makes You Feel Good* by Todd Parr
- *The Old Women Who Loved to Read* by John Winch
- *I Read Signs* by Tana Hoban
- *Jeremiah Learns to Read* by Jo Ellen Bogart (illustrated by Laura Fernandez and Rick Jacobson)
- *Wednesday's Surprise* by Eve Bunting (illustrated by Donald Carrick)
- *Read Me a Book* by Barbara Reid
- *You Read to Me, I'll Read to You: Very Short Stories to Read Together* by Mary Ann Hoberman (illustrated by Michael Emberley)
- *Book!* by Kristine O'Connell George (illustrated by Maggie Smith)
- *A Bedtime Story* by Mem Fox (illustrated by Elivia Savadier)
- *Read to Your Bunny* (Max and Ruby series) by Rosemary Wells
- *I Took My Frog to the Library* by Eric A. Kimmel
- *Wild About Books* by Judy Sierra (illustrated by Marc Brown)

It can also be effective to begin the year with no books in the Reading centre. This practice may seem unusual, but the purpose is to ensure that the children have a meaningful connection with every book available. This connection will make the children feel successful and make them want to visit the centre.

Books for the Reading centre

We rarely put a book in the Reading centre without sharing it first with the large group. Doing this encouraged the children to respond, "We read that book all together this morning, and I can read it myself now!" The Reading centre filled up with books quickly since we read several times a day, adding each new title along with multiple copies when available.

After each read-aloud, we invited a child to place the book in the Reading centre. This practice afforded us an opportunity to reinforce where the centre was located, how to handle the books, and how to put the books away. For example, we might choose to place the books on the shelves upright, with covers facing out, or put softcover books in the appropriate bin and hardcover books on the shelf. In order to keep this centre inviting, we regularly added books borrowed from the library/resource centre or other teachers.

Favorite Author Table

A typical Favorite Author Table has a sign prominently displaying the featured author's name and about half a dozen books by the author. In the case of Bernard Waber, author of the Lyle the Crocodile stories, adding a plastic and a plush crocodile to the tabletop would be appropriate.

Creating a "Favorite Author Table" in the Reading centre is a good idea. By doing so, you can heighten the children's awareness of and interest in the works of different authors and illustrators. Frank Asch and Mem Fox are wonderful authors to feature at such a table. They have written a number of simple and inviting books that appeal to young children. Authors such as Lucy Cousins and A. J. Rey have approved the production of materials related to their books — for example, puzzles, compact discs, models, games, and puppets — and these items can be added to this table to encourage the children to retell the stories and relate to the characters in them. A photograph of the author can also be added.

It is important that all books and related materials be read aloud and discussed in the large group before being added to the Favorite Author Table. The teacher can also take a large-group opportunity to use a SMART Board to research information about the author (e.g., country, family, and interests). Introducing author resources in the large group serves to motivate the children to revisit and use these items at the table, thereby furthering their language learning.

Here is a list of more authors whose titles work well at a Favorite Author Table.

Janet and Allan Ahlberg	Pat Hutchins
Byron Barton	Ann Jonas
Marion Dane Bauer	Ezra Jack Keats
Ann Blades	Leo Lionni
Paulette Bourgeois	Helen Oxenbury
Anthony Browne	Patricia Polacco
Eric Carle	Barbara Reid
Donald Crews	Nancy Tafuri
Tomie dePaola	Max Velthuijs
Lois Ehlert	Bernard Waber
Phoebe Gilman	Rosemary Wells
Kevin Henkes	Brian Wildsmith
Eric Hill	Harriet Ziefert
Tana Hoban	

Books for other centres

The Reading centre should not be the only space where reading materials are available. We always introduced reading materials at all the other centres for the children to use in a meaningful way, for example, water books at the Water centre, building books at the Construction centre, and family stories at the Home/Dramatic Play centre. All of these practices help children love books and spend many happy hours making their own reading choices.

Favorite Books of Different Kinds

The following is a list of our favorite books to read throughout the year and then add to the Reading centre for children to read.

Wordless Books

Reading wordless books is invaluable in exposing children to plot development and sense of story. When sharing these books, the teacher tells the story by describing what is happening in the pictures. The teacher may also elicit suggestions and predictions from the children as they examine each picture. For example the teacher might ask, "What do you think the author is trying to tell us here?"
- *Good Night, Gorilla* by Peggy Rathmann
- *Hug* by Jez Alborough
- *Look Again!* by Tana Hoban
- *Is It Larger? Is It Smaller?* by Tana Hoban
- *Carl Goes Shopping* by Alexandra Day
- *Changes, Changes* by Pat Hutchins
- *Peter Spier's Rain* by Peter Spier
- *Snowman* by Raymond Briggs

- *Home* by Jeannie Baker
- *Have You Seen My Duckling?* by Nancy Tafuri

Simple Fiction Books

- *A Good Day* by Kevin Henkes
- *Silly Little Goose!* by Nancy Tafuri
- *In the Tall, Tall Grass* by Denise Fleming
- *In the Small, Small Pond* by Denise Fleming
- *Coco Can't Wait* by Taro Gomi
- *Time for Bed* by Mem Fox (illustrated by Jane Dyer)
- *The Chick and the Duckling* by Mirra Ginsburg (translated from the Russian of V. Suteyev; illustrated by Jose Aruego and Ariane Dewey)
- *A Dark Dark Tale* by Ruth Brown
- *Shoes from Grandpa* by Mem Fox (illustrated by Jane Dyer)

Storybooks

- *Bark, George* by Jules Feiffer
- *Amazing Grace* by Mary Hoffman (illustrated by Caroline Binch)
- *Ahmed's Secret* by Florence Parry Heide and Judith Heide Gilliland
- *Sami and the Time of the Troubles* by Florence Parry Heide and Judith Heide Gilliland
- *Jazzy in the Jungle* by Lucy Cousins
- *Hue Boy* by Rita Phillips Mitchell (illustrated by Caroline Binch)
- *Mrs. Katz and Tush* by Patricia Polacco

Non-fiction Books

- *Short, Tall, Big or Small?* by Kari Jenson Gold
- *Patterns Everywhere* by Kari Jenson Gold
- *Count!* by Denise Fleming
- *Snow; Sticks; Stones,* all by PlayBac (EyeLike Nature series)

Books with Interesting Formats

It is important to introduce children to a range of book formats so they learn to understand that books can be full of wonderful surprises.
- *Something from Nothing* by Phoebe Gilman (story within a story)
- *Papa, Please Get the Moon for Me* by Eric Carle (story with fold-outs)
- *The Wide-Mouthed Frog* by Keith Faulkner (story with pop-ups and large font)
- Spot books by Eric Hill (story in lift-the-flap format)
- *Rhinos for Lunch and Elephants for Supper! — A Maasai Tale* by Tololwa M. Mollel (illustrated by Barbara Spurll) (story with a detailed border around each page)
- *Tickle the Duck!* by Ethan Long (story with touch-and-feel pages)
- *The Mitten* by Jan Brett (story within a story)

Setting Up and Maintaining the Reading Centre

Here is a workable outline for the physical setup of a Reading centre.

- Ideally, the centre would have a good-sized space complete with a rocking chair, carpet, cuddly toys, and pillows to encourage the children to browse, listen to stories read aloud, read to each other, and imitate more successful readers.
- Be sure to provide a wide variety of bias-free books in good condition. It is important that the books represent many different genres and forms, as well as different cultures, races, and linguistic groups. *Cleversticks* by Bernard Ashley and *The Name Jar* by Yangsook Choi are two examples.
- Frequently change the collection, perhaps once a month or when necessary.
- Use a movable, open, book-shelving unit that allows you to display books attractively with the cover of many showing.
- Provide a station where children can listen to audiobooks while following text. Children love to discover that their teacher is reading the story, so consider making your own audiobooks; otherwise, purchase commercial materials. *Note:* Be careful not to break copyright. We suggest recording only those stories that do not already have a commercial recording.
- Provide materials such as markers, pencils, happy face stickers, Post-it notes, small note pads, and bookmarks that will allow children to record degree of enjoyment, write notes, or draw pictures about the books they like or dislike. Their reviews can be posted on a board in the Reading centre.

Remember to demonstrate with the whole group how to show opinions of different books, for example, a happy face for like, a sad face for dislike.

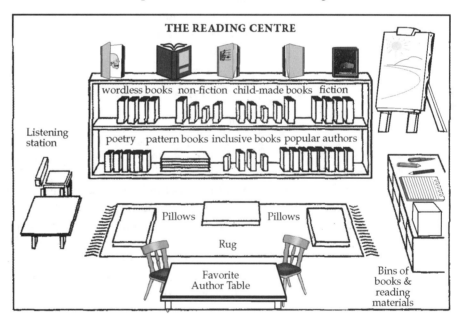

THE READING CENTRE

wordless books non-fiction child-made books fiction

poetry pattern books inclusive books popular authors

Listening station

Pillows Pillows

Rug

Favorite Author Table

Bins of books & reading materials

The Reading centre is the repository of both published and child-made books. Titles introduced and read at Gathering Time are usually moved to this centre so children can enjoy them further.

Literacy Activities for the Reading Centre

The Reading centre itself serves as an effective vehicle in the development of children's literacy skills and a positive attitude towards reading. The carefully selected books that are available provide opportunities to understand letters and sounds, learn about the directionality of print, and develop a bank of sight words. The books also offer children the opportunity to enjoy the magic of stories. The children may giggle at the pictures they see, share a story with a friend, and relate the books they are exposed to to their lives and the wider community. The Reading centre provides a comfortable environment where the act of reading is fun and enjoyable.

This literacy learning can be further extended by providing related activities and challenges to the Reading centre. The following activities have been successfully used in various Kindergarten Reading centres to meet the needs of a wide range of learners. Many of these activities typically begin at a Gathering Time or at a permanent centre other than the Reading centre. During the activity period, the children work at the appropriate centre. For example, they might help to make an A B C book at the Drawing/Writing centre. When they complete such a book or other project, such as a game or sentence strips, the resources are transferred to the Reading centre for child use.

Exploring Environmental Print

For many young learners, the first experience with reading is the understanding of various familiar symbols, pictures, and logos in the everyday community and environment. For example, many children read the Stop sign at the end of the street or a favorite neighborhood restaurant sign or the local gas station logo long before they read the formal print in a book. Educators refer to this familiar text as *environmental print* and teachers can capitalize on this natural interest and use it to engage children in the world of reading. Not only does this environmental print help develop sound–symbol connections, but it helps young learners to see themselves as readers and develop confidence in their abilities. Confidence is paramount!

"Of Course, You Know How to Read!"

On the first day of Kindergarten, we would gather the class into the large group to say, "You are all so clever and I know that you can read!"

The responses were always varied. Some children were positive, saying, "I love to read, and I read with my brother every day!" Others were less confident, saying, "I don't know how to read." We refuted this assessment by saying, "Of course, you know how to read!"

We would then pull out an empty Cheerios cereal box. The children happily and proudly chimed in, saying, "Cheerios" or "cereal."

We smiled proudly and said: "You said that you couldn't read. You *can* read and you are correct. It says 'Cheerios' right here!" We then pointed to the word on the box.

We asked the children, "How did you know this says 'Cheerios'?" We then drew their attention to the pictures, colors, and first letter.

We continued by pulling out a Smarties box and asking, "What does this say?" The class usually cried out, "Smarties" or "candy," and again we reinforced their reading.

This exercise continued with a Tide box, a yogurt container, an apple juice box, and many other pieces of familiar environmental print. We quickly made believers of them all. They saw themselves as readers and

---

understood that we valued the many reading skills they already had. Together, we had set the stage that "we are all readers" and that we were going to learn to read many new things together.

An excellent way to help children make connections is to follow up on the discussion by reading a title such as *The Signmaker's Assistant* by Tedd Arnold. This hilarious story includes a great deal of environmental print. It explores what the world would be like without essential signs.

In our classrooms, we first had a group discussion and then prompted the children to search at home for things that they could read. We directed them to the kitchen, laundry room, and bathroom and asked them to bring their boxes to school the following day. To support this request, we sent home a short letter to parents explaining our environmental print focus and enlisting their support. A sample letter follows.

Dear Parents/Guardians,

Memorizing familiar print is one way that children acquire reading skills and develop confidence in themselves as young readers. All the familiar print in the environment can be very helpful with this learning.

Has your child ever noticed a Stop sign while you are driving, pointed to a favorite cereal in the grocery store, or asked to go to a family restaurant after seeing its logo? When your child notices such text, he or she is making meaning of the print in the environment — an extremely exciting process! Teachers call this "reading environmental print" and recognize it as an effective way to help children dive into reading.

In your child's class, the children have been examining various pieces of environmental print, including cookie boxes, toothpaste tubes, and candy wrappers. All of these familiar pieces of text have been posted in the classroom under a sign, "Look What We Can Read." The children are all excited about their reading.

At home, please encourage your child to look in the playroom, kitchen, bathroom, and laundry room for boxes and packages with text that he or she can read. Remind your child to bring such items to school and we will add them to the wall. We will use items on this Environmental Print Wall in a number of ways: to identify letters, discuss letter sounds, recognize upper and lower case letters, and discuss the number of letters in each word.

In the coming weeks, the children will be sorting all of these pieces of environmental print, perhaps creating a "Toothpaste Book," a "Cereal Book," or a "Cracker Book." They will also be making a co-operative A B C book with the items and using a Concentration game and puzzle. We will take an opportunity to use these boxes and packages to discuss the importance of recycling and reusing materials, too.

Watch for the books of Tana Hoban when you are visiting our classroom or looking at Borrow-a-Book program titles. Tana Hoban, an accomplished children's author and illustrator, has published many non-fiction books that include photographs of print in the environment. You may also want to search for these books at your local library. As for the class, we will be going on walks in our community and taking photographs of signs and logos so that we can create a class book modelled on Ms. Hoban's work.

Sincerely,

We also dedicated a large bulletin board to this environmental print focus, ideally using a space in the Reading centre. Children worked in a small group to make a sign that read "Look What We Can Read." As the children brought in items from home, they presented them to the class; we then cut the front of the boxes off and posted them on the bulletin board for the children to view.

Here was an opportunity for us to point out different styles of print and font, as well as capital and lower case letters: "These are both the letter *a* but one is a capital and one is a lower case. How are they different? Let's try to make some in the air with a finger."

Once the children had brought in many items and filled the board, there was a huge set of resources to use to help bridge the gap between the familiar environmental print and the conventional print that appears in books. When the environmental print display had had time to be admired and absorbed by the children, maybe several weeks, the items were taken down and used in some of the following ways to extend the learning.

Making books of boxes

Sort a selection of the environmental print items into various categories, such as cereals, toothpastes, toys, crackers, and cookies; then, cut off the front of the boxes, mount them on construction paper, and use a three-hole punch and rings to assemble them into a simple book. Have the children suggest titles and vote to determine the most appropriate title for each book, for example, "The Toothpaste Book" or "Our Favorite Kinds of Cookies." Have the children who brought the boxes to school write their names on the back of the boxes in permanent marker, indicating that they are the "experts" when it comes to reading those boxes in the book. That way, when the children are independently reading the book in the Reading centre, they can search out the "expert" for assistance, if necessary. What a natural way to build confidence!

Making an A B C book with logos and labels

Use some pieces from the environmental print collection to create an A B C book. Assemble 26 pieces of strong cardboard and label each piece with one of the letters from A to Z. Cut out some of the familiar logos and place them on the appropriate page. For example, you could paste a milk bag to the *M* page, while adding a raisin box to the *R* page. Pages featuring less common letters, such as *Q* or *X*, might remain blank.

Consider making this alphabet book a co-operative class activity. The book could be created as a Big Book by using large pieces of bristol board for the pages. This format would permit reading to the class during large-group times. The book could then be added to the Reading centre for small groups to enjoy during activity time.

As an alternative, let children follow the same process to create individual A B C books. Grocery store flyers are useful for this activity. It is important to read many alphabet books, to familiarize the children with upper and lower case letters, as well as the varying formats that have been used by illustrators to present the letters.

Creating a matching game

Select a small number of items from the environmental print collection — 10 is recommended — and cut them into the same size and shape. Mount these logos onto hard cardboard and then use similar blank cards to write the corresponding words. For example, if one label was Dove soap, then in large, clear, primary print, write *Dove* on the corresponding card. Once 10 sets of matching cards have been created, you will have a Concentration game with 20 cards.

By printing these familiar logos and labels in conventional print, you are removing the picture and color cues that initially assisted the children in reading the text. Doing this is using what the children already know to extend their understanding and developing literacy skills. When playing the game, the children will be able to use the familiar logo to help make a match: "I know these are the same because they both say *d - o - v - e* and those are the same letters."

Providing homemade puzzles

Select a large logo from the environmental print collection, cut it into random, irregular pieces, and laminate or cover the pieces in clear tape to create a homemade puzzle. The children can use puzzles like this during the Literacy and the Arts activity period to practise problem solving and reassembling the text.

Try making several different puzzles. You can keep them organized by gluing the pieces of each puzzle onto a different colored paper, so they can be easily sorted for assembly or tidy up. Store the individual puzzles in large Ziploc bags that can be labelled with the name in conventional print. Doing this will provide a further opportunity to compare and match texts.

Exploring Tana Hoban books

Tana Hoban is a children's author and illustrator who primarily features photographs. These photographs are of common environmental signs and symbols such as road and construction signs with familiar words, shapes, and colors. Visit your school or local library and borrow a selection of these books, so that the children can use their previous knowledge of environmental print to "read" them. These books can be put on display at the Favorite Author Table and in that way the children will have an opportunity to recognize and sort the books from the other texts in the Reading centre. A child might say: "This book doesn't belong on the regular shelf. It's a Tana Hoban book so it goes on the Favorite Author Table." (See the letter on page 61.)

Looking for signs

Plan to take the children on a walk around the school's local community to identify various familiar signs. Before walking, ask the children to predict the signs and symbols they might see. Record their ideas on a large piece of chart paper and use this list as a reference upon your return. ("Which signs did we see?" "Which signs didn't we see?")

While on the walk, take photographs of the environmental print that the children are able to identify. Perhaps they will see a school sign, a Stop sign, a street sign, a pizza restaurant sign, a corner store sign, a local park sign, and a parking sign. These photographs can be developed and placed in a photo album and then added to the Reading centre. On the page opposite each photograph, write the word in conventional print so that the children can examine both forms when reading the album in the Reading centre.

Working with Different Kinds of Texts

Teachers can introduce children to the world of literacy by using different kinds of texts. The patterns, rhythms, rhymes, lyrics, and connections found in these different types of texts help children to develop an awareness of the richness of language.

Sentence strips from pattern books

Simple pattern books are an integral part of any Reading centre, and beginning readers successfully use these books to memorize text. While committing some text to memory is a necessary stage in reading development, young readers can be encouraged to further develop their skills by more readily focusing on the text. Write the text from a familiar pattern book onto sentence strips with one sentence on each strip. Challenge the children to reassemble the text and then read the strips without using the book and illustrations for assistance.

We suggest numbering these sentence strips on the back, so that children can more independently check their accuracy. The strips can easily be sequenced on the floor or at a table, but a pocket chart can also be effective — such charts make storage easy too. *Cat on the Mat* by Brian Wildsmith can be effective text for an activity with sentence strips.

A child has cut out, ordered, and glued strips of text onto construction paper and added animal images.

Recommended Poets

Sonja Dunn
Sheree Fitch
Dennis Lee
Jack Prelutsky
Shel Silverstein
Judith Viorst

Poetry every day

Poetry is an effective way to teach children to read and develop an awareness of rhyme and sight vocabulary. Try introducing a new poem each week and read it to the class several times daily. Valuable resources include *The Random House*

Book of Poetry, compiled by Jack Prelutsky (illustrated by Arnold Lobel); *The Bill Martin Jr. Big Book of Poetry*, by various authors; and *Here's a Little Poem: A Very First Book of Poetry*, compiled by Jane Yolen and Andrew Fusek Peters (illustrated by Polly Dunbar). Help children make connections to their learning by relating the poem to a specific centre or area of learning in the classroom; for example, if there are farm animals at the Sand centre, the poem "The Giving Farm" by Vicki Witcher would be appropriate. You might share an appropriate poem about reading or one about an upcoming season, or search the Internet to find a simple children's poem that captures the interest of the class.

Provide the children with a visual aid. Write the poem on large chart paper and add appropriate illustrations beside particular words. Doing so allows the children to follow along as they chant, and that helps them to learn that the printed letters and words on the page comprise the text that holds the message. After reading and chanting the poem as much as desired, add it to the wall in the Reading centre. Give children an opportunity to read it on the wall at the centre and find particular words and letters with a pointer or ruler. You can later mount it on a large piece of construction paper, fold it, and add it to a Poetry basket for children to revisit.

It is also a good idea to send these poems home weekly. Be sure to print them in the largest font that will still let you keep the poetry lines intact. Ask the parents to listen to their children read the poem. Have the parents store the poems in a binder that will be kept at home. That way, the children can add a new poem each week and revisit these familiar poems regularly. Doing so will help develop sight vocabulary and fluency, and the children will be proud to show how they can read a piece of writing from school.

You can easily extend this activity for the children able to read these poems independently. Type the poem in an easy-to-read font and then cut it into sentence strips for the children to reassemble and glue onto another piece of paper. To heighten the challenge for the more advanced readers, you could further cut the sentence strips into individual words. The children could also draw illustrations to accompany the reassembled poems.

Songs and Rhymes: Similarly, all these poem activities could be replicated with familiar class songs and nursery rhymes such as "Twinkle, Twinkle," "Row, Row, Row Your Boat," and "The More We Get Together." These songs and rhymes can be recorded on large chart paper for Shared Reading and then added to the Reading centre in a Song basket or as "Our Songbook."

Using text sets

Young learners need to know how to think critically, question, and make connections between ideas. Teachers can help them develop these skills naturally through their thoughtful and systematic selection of reading materials. Books that are somehow related or connected are considered *text sets* and these can be an important part of any Kindergarten Reading centre. Books in a text set may be based on an author, illustrator, plot, setting, character, theme, or idea.

Discussing the similarities and differences between these books can help children to think more deeply and tangentially. For example, a child might observe, "*Happy Birthday, Moon* and *Papa, Please Get the Moon for Me* are both books about the moon." Discussing will also help them make real and meaningful connections between books, between themselves and books, and between books and the world around them. For example, a child might say, "*Wild About Books* reminds me of the library where I go to pick my books; however, there aren't any animals there."

These weekly poems can also be typed and added to a binder or Duotang titled "Our Class Poetry Book."

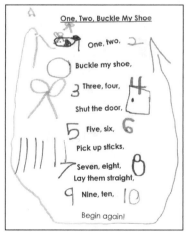

After chanting and reading "One, Two, Buckle My Shoe," a child named Jake was challenged to reassemble it by sequencing each line.

Reading different versions of the same story — fairy tales, for example — provides an opportunity to listen carefully, make observations, and compare and contrast the text in the various books. When teachers read these books aloud to the large group, children can readily develop their listening and oral language skills by responding to this question: "How are these books different?"

The following chart will aid in understanding the value of reading children a set of related books.

Making Sense of Text Sets	
Common Characteristic	**Learning**
Same author	Understanding personal writing style (For example: "Paulette Bourgeois always begins her Franklin books in this way: 'Franklin could count by twos and tie his shoes.' ")
Same illustrator	Recognizing various illustrative techniques (For example: "Barbara Reid creates all her illustrations with Plasticine.")
Similar character	Recognizing that writing can be created by different authors and have different forms, but may still include similar characters (For example: "This book has a bear as the main character, and this poem is about a bear too, but they look very different.")
Same setting	Understanding the setting as the place where a story takes place (For example: "This first story is at the beach, and in this second book, the girl wants to build a sandcastle at the beach.")
Same genre	Identifying characteristics and features of various kinds of texts (For example: "Poems don't go all across the line; sometimes they rhyme and sometimes they don't.")
Same story	Identifying subtle differences between two or more versions of the same basic story (For example: "In this version of 'The Three Little Pigs' . . .")

We recommend having a specific bin in the Reading centre to house the text set books. This bin might contain only a few books, even just two. Before being added to the Reading centre for children to use independently, all of these texts would be read aloud to the class and discussed.

Responding to Their Reading

Children's responses to reading can include choosing and voting for favorite titles, compiling individual words for a class dictionary, and volunteering to read familiar books aloud to others. Such activities promote literacy learning at and beyond the Reading centre.

Choosing favorites

As part of their literacy development, children need frequent, meaningful opportunities to express their opinions about the books that they read and have heard read aloud. Teachers often ask children to describe, draw, or write about a favorite part in a story. Sometimes, children use a symbol of a happy, sad, or neutral face to indicate their feelings about a book.

The Chick and the Duckling

😊	😐	☹
SaVaJ	Adam	PaKota
KaTy	samie	JT
MAX		KeegaN
JoSH		LiNDSa
RRRR	rr rr	
SaMMy		
JORDaN		

On this voting chart, children in the class indicated their opinion of a picture book.

Children can also express their opinions about texts in other ways, such as making a concrete graph. Ask the children to stand in lines labelled with the following headings: "I loved that book," "I liked that book," "I was not fond of that book." The children in the various lines will gain a chance to share ideas with like-minded classmates and then report back to the large group. The number of children in each line can also be compared and contrasted — most, least, how many more, how many fewer.

Have the children vote on their favorite. You might select two or three different books and lean them up against a whiteboard or chalkboard. Draw a chart above the books and write, "Which book do you like best?" Have each child print his or her name above the book preferred. Tally the results which can then be discussed and compared. This activity is also a good way to introduce children to the concept of voting and the idea of voting only once.

In order to use large-group time most effectively, you could introduce this activity to the large group and then direct the children to cast their votes during the next activity period. The results can then be tabulated and discussed at Gathering Time. This approach avoids children sitting passively, watching their peers as they write on the voting chart.

Compiling a class dictionary

Many commercial, primary picture dictionaries are available and very useful in the Kindergarten classroom. The combination of words and illustrations makes them appealing for children to examine in the Reading centre.

This interest can be extended by working co-operatively as a class to create a "Class Dictionary." Assemble 27 pages, one for each letter of the alphabet and one for the cover, and systematically add words and accompanying illustrations to the appropriate pages. Since the class will be adding words continually, you might want to make the dictionary an oversized book of bristol board intended to last the entire year.

Begin by adding the names of the children in the class and then add other words as they become important to the children. Focusing on familiar nouns, as opposed to little high-frequency words such as *the*, *is*, or *and*, can be most effective. Although high-frequency words are important, they do not conjure up an image in the child's mind the way nouns do; therefore, they cannot be easily accompanied by a supportive illustration. Words such as *gym*, *library*, *music*, and *school* are meaningful additions that will regularly appear in the Daily Message (see Chapter 2). Key classroom words such as *sand*, *water*, and *big blocks* can also be effectively included.

This class dictionary can serve as a meaningful alternative to a word wall, something that is difficult to include in a small classroom where wall space is at a premium. It's important to maintain ample room to display and celebrate the children's artwork and photographs of their work, as well as visual and anchor charts such as brainstorming lists, poems, and songs.

This class dictionary will be a frequently visited addition to the Reading centre, but it can also be useful at the Drawing/Writing centre when more advanced literacy learners are recording their ideas and need to refer to this resource.

Signing up to read

After visiting the Reading centre many times and doing various simple, reading-related activities, children become more confident as beginning readers. Kindergarten children will often approach the teacher, happily asking, "Can I read you this book? I can read it all by myself." To capitalize on this interest, you might want to set up an "I Would Like to Read to the Class" sheet. Once the children feel comfortable reading a book, they can sign up and wait for an opportunity to read it aloud to the class during group time.

I would like to read to the class	
Name	Book Title
Adam	Clifford
ALEXA	Caton Mat
JACKSON	I ♥ BOATS

Students sign up to read aloud. The same simple format can be adapted for expressing interest in reading to the principal.

When children read a book to the class, it opens up several possibilities for learning. Children gain a wonderful opportunity to reinforce their reading skills, as well as to help develop their group presentation abilities and confidence. The teacher can point out the importance of using a clear, loud voice and of appropriately holding the book so all of the audience can see the illustrations. More advanced readers can even work on adding volume and expression to their voices when reading aloud to the class.

When the teacher reads aloud to the class, modelling this appropriate behavior and emphasizing these presentation skills become important. The teacher may want to intentionally make presentation mistakes and model their correction. For example, if she is holding the book so that some children cannot see the pictures, she might comment, "Oh, I better turn a little, so that you can all see."

Once this reading sign-up sheet becomes successful, this activity could be extended by approaching the principal and vice-principal to see whether a few children could come to the office, once a week at a designated time, to share their developing reading skill. Introduce a similar sign-up sheet, "I Would Like to Read to the Principal." The teacher-librarian or other designated staff may want to join in the celebration of reading.

Creating an Environment for Success in the Reading Centre

The following section is presented in terms of questions that the reflective practitioner is encouraged to ask about the classroom's Reading centre. The answers reflect what we have found to be best practices.

1. How do I ensure that the centre remains inviting and bias free?

- Change the books regularly, culling books that are worn, biased, or no longer of interest to the children.
- Borrow new books from the library/resource centre or a colleague.
- Purposely select books to support children's interests (e.g., bugs and marine animals) and to reflect different gender roles, languages, and cultures (e.g., celebrations such as Passover and Kwanza).
- Highlight favorite and award-winning authors and illustrators through a Favorite Author Table and during group read-alouds.
- Add multiple copies of favorite read-aloud texts or stories. For example, our students liked *Rosie's Walk* by Pat Hutchins.

2. How do I ensure that the books are efficiently organized so children and adults can easily find what they want?

- Arrange the books according to an appropriate sorting system (e.g., by genre, topic, or type of cover — hard or soft).
- Stand up some books for display, perhaps using small easel stands, to better invite the children to select those titles.
- Create a Text Set Bin to house the books that belong to a particular text set (e.g., all the books that feature ducks).

3. How do I ensure that the children use this centre regularly?

- Make this centre one of the choices available to the children during the Literacy and the Arts activity period. This centre is an integral part of the literacy program, not something to be enjoyed just when "real" work is completed.
- Schedule yourself to spend time here during the Literacy and the Arts activity period, reading and talking with the children about their selections.
- Provide large blocks of time for literacy activities. For example, a period of 45 minutes to an hour should be sufficient.
- Before adding a book to the Reading centre, be sure to read it during a group time. We found that doing this provided a context for the children's reading.
- Add multiple copies of books that you have shared at the read-aloud time. For example, you might read a Big Book, such as *Cookie's Week* by Cindy Ward (illustrated by Tomie dePaola), and then add several small copies to the

Reading centre for the children's use. (We found it valuable to read this story several times before adding it to the Reading centre — children need to hear a story many times before they will feel comfortable enough to try to read it for themselves.)

4. How do I ensure that the children have multiple experiences with books each day?

- Read aloud to the large group several times each day. A read-aloud time may be as short as a poem or as long as a fiction book read over several sessions.
- Schedule a quiet reading time each day so the children can look at books independently. At the beginning of the year, this session may last only 5 or 10 minutes. Its length will increase throughout the year.
- Partner with older classes for a weekly Reading Buddy experience.
- During the Literacy and the Arts activity period, set aside a few moments to conference individually. Prioritize, but be realistic. You might want to schedule four children to read each period, perhaps at the Reading centre, at your chair, or at a conference table.

Mileposts to Help Guide Teacher Observations of Children Reading

The developmental mileposts outlined here are guidelines only — they are not intended to be all-inclusive or prescriptive. They can be very useful in helping teachers assess children's developmental levels, plan appropriate demonstrations, and offer timely feedback. We used them for observation and assessment and to plan effective teaching strategies in the Kindergarten classroom.

How children show interest in books

Children might show active interest in books in any of the following concrete ways:

- voluntarily looking at books
- taking on the role of a reader with other children and favorite toys
- asking for favorite stories to be read
- pointing out illustrations and labels
- reading environmental print, such as *Shell* and *Parking*
- pointing at the pictures and making up their own stories
- noticing when parts are changed or left out
- repeating stories from memory
- borrowing books to share with family members
- selecting the Reading centre as an activity during the Literacy and the Arts activity period
- talking about book preferences, authors, and illustrators
- linking books together; commenting on similar subject matter, authors, or illustrations; and making connections to the real world (For example: "That book reminds me of another book about dogs. I used to have a dog, but he got old and died.")

The knowledge that children have about books

Children learn that there are established ways of approaching books and that print and pictures both carry meaning. They might know any of the following:

- that books are held right side up
- that pages in a storybook are turned carefully from front to back of the book
- that the table of contents helps the reader find things in a non-fiction book
- that print in English goes from left to right, from top to bottom
- that texts have features such as title, author's name, illustrator's name (if there is one), and dedication
- that print holds meaning
- that pictures help to tell the story or explain the print
- that sounds and letters have a relationship
- that fiction and non-fiction books are read differently
- that print and pictures are different
- that there are different kinds of print (e.g., magazines and picture books)

The skills and strategies that children use

Children might apply any of the following reading skills and strategies:

- reading their names in a different context
- reading the names of others such as siblings and peers
- recognizing environmental print
- making up their own versions of familiar stories using the pictures
- reading simple picture books (e.g., *Have You Seen My Duckling?* by Nancy Tafuri)
- memorizing simple, familiar texts that have a strong pattern and a good relationship between the pictures and the text (e.g., *I Went Walking* by Sue Williams)
- chiming in with some words from familiar stories
- reading simple, one-word text from picture books (e.g., *Snow* by PlayBac)
- reading books that have a strong pattern or rhyme (e.g., *Where's Spot?* by Eric Hill)
- reading books where the print is different on every page, but much of the text is either repetitive or has a consistent rhyme (e.g., *Cookie's Week* by Cindy Ward, with its excellent correlation between pictures and text)
- skipping words they don't know
- using pictures as clues to read new text
- using the structure of the sentence to read unfamiliar text
- using knowledge of the sounds of letters to check approximations for new words
- rereading parts of the text when the meaning is lost
- using the title, subheadings, and table of contents to find specific information when reading non-fiction
- using different reading strategies to read different genres (For example, in expository text, the reader begins and ends reading in varying places and reads in chunks, using headings and the table of contents to decide which portions of the text to read.)

The Reading centre is a dynamic and ever changing repository of books and other print resources. Here the children can find commercial books of all kinds as well as books that they and their friends have created. These resources are first introduced, celebrated, and used for teaching times during large-group gatherings. In the inviting setting of the Reading centre, the children can then reread, look at, listen to, and enjoy the texts on their own or share reading with a friend.

5

The Visual Arts Centre

The Visual Arts centre provides children with many opportunities to imagine, create, dramatize, and communicate their ideas and feelings. It is a dynamic, never static centre, demanding a regular infusion of new and inviting materials and artistic techniques. It can become very messy; therefore, routines and organization are important. At this centre, paint, glue, found materials, and modelling materials are available together so that the children can problem-solve and combine them in interesting, creative, and unique ways.

The Visual Arts centre also plays an integral part in the acquisition of literacy.

When they draw, paint, glue, and model, children naturally use oral language to describe, retell, relate, reflect, question, label, and problem-solve. In order to promote this literacy learning, teachers must provide children with open-ended art opportunities rather than the more traditional teacher-directed arts and craft activities.

Open-Ended Versus Teacher-Directed Art

In some Kindergarten classrooms, teachers are tempted to provide pre-cut patterns, stencils, or teacher-directed crafts for the children to use at the Visual Arts centre. These teachers find it particularly tempting to do this around holidays or celebrations such as Mother's Day when there may be some pressure for children to give gifts. We suggest that teachers always consider the suitability of giving such gifts. If the gift giving seems appropriate, then let the children select what the gift might be: a card, a drawing, a poem, a photograph, or a recording.

Teachers who believe that all the children should participate and make identical gifts offer several reasons in support of this widespread idea. They say they expect that, since the children are much the same age, they should be able to produce the same recognizable product. Some contend that the children can't think of ways to create recognizable products and need the teacher's pattern, direction, and thinking in order to do so. Others argue that the children like to be given a model to copy. Many teachers also tell us that they follow this practice because the parents expect and like it.

From our experience, however, we understand that demanding the same product can be destructive. Doing so can frustrate children, limit their creativity, and erode their confidence as learners. Teacher-imposed activities often result in children saying, "I can't do it," "I'm not good at art," or "Teacher, can you draw a castle for me?" Despite their similar chronological age, children are at many different places on the learning continuum. Those who are at the manipulative stage of drawing are frustrated because they can't produce the model, for example, a caterpillar out of an egg carton. Since the children cannot identify or envision the relationship between the concrete object and the abstract symbol, such an activity requires the teacher to do the work. Other children are able to see this relationship and have much more inventive ways of implementing their ideas than following the teacher's model.

Considering the outcomes to be achieved

When planning activities, teachers are wise to ask themselves: "Who is actively engaged in the thinking, problem solving, doing, and learning? Is it me, the teacher, or the children?" We always asked ourselves these questions. If the work is teacher prepared, it sets up many children to fail and denies all the children an opportunity to learn through exploration, experience, and meaningful instruction.

If we "do" for children in one area of the curriculum such as visual arts, the children will expect us to "do" for them in all areas, including reading, writing, and mathematics. We will create children who will not take risks or explore the limits of their own potential, children who will have a low image of themselves as learners.

In our experience, the only children to show any enjoyment in copying the teacher's work are those who wish to please or who may be afraid to risk and think for themselves. When asked, children are well aware of who did the work and the thinking. Some feel uncomfortable taking credit for the work and often say, "My teacher helped me with these parts." For many others, copying the teacher's work means tears, a refusal to try, frustration, and minimal effort. As Brian Cambourne suggests, when learners see no relevance in a task or lack ownership of it, they disengage and withdraw from the learning.

Parents need to understand that despite the absence of perfectly finished crafts and products, their children are still learning. Teachers can inform, educate, and reassure them about this. We have important, but different roles to play in the children's learning. Rather than providing set patterns to copy, adults need to help children to take risks and develop their own ways to represent the world. Parents and teachers need to respond positively to all their children's best efforts. We do not suggest that low standards be accepted, only that the expectations fit the children's individual abilities.

In any Kindergarten classroom, it is counterproductive to expect the children to copy the teacher's ideas — children will have a wide range of developmental levels and abilities. Rather, we should expect that the children's creations will represent their varied thinking, competencies, and interests. Our role is much more than searching through the latest craft magazines or Internet for cute art ideas. When we observe the need and interest of the children, we offer a wide variety of techniques, for example, scoring and curling paper. We also demonstrate how to mix colors and choose different paints/dyes that support their work. We are always available to help the children solve the problems they encounter. By expecting different results, we set the stage for children to take risks and think creatively.

The chart on the next page helps to clarify the differences between a teacher-directed task and a child-directed task.

Teacher-Directed Task	Child-Directed Task
emphasizes product	emphasizes process
tends to be neat	tends to be messy
frustrates some/many	satisfies all
tends to be based on adults' perception of the world	based on child's perception of the world
involves little or no risk	involves risk
requires little imagination	requires imagination and creative thinking
provides no problems to solve	provides many problems to solve
erodes confidence	builds confidence
promotes copying	fosters originality
offers only one solution	encourages many solutions
encourages negative judgments	encourages positive judgments
expects each product to be the same	expects and promotes different products
lacks creative thinking	promotes creative thinking

The goals we set always help children to extend, consolidate, and apply their learning. *We focus on the process, not the finished product.* All work is valued and expected to be individualized and different. Giving children a pre-cut pattern, such as a gingerbread man for them to decorate, denies them the opportunity to create their own shape.

All children in a Kindergarten classroom are expected to support each other no matter their stage of development. We frequently overheard more competent artists reassuring others by saying, "I used to draw like that, and then I did it this way." Children thrive in such a positive atmosphere.

In our Kindergarten classrooms, the Visual Arts centre serves a dual purpose. First, children are always encouraged to follow their own interests, for example, to paint a picture about their family, make a box sculpture of their cat, make a pizza with the playdough, or just experiment with the materials provided. Second, children are encouraged to use the materials provided to support the learning at the other centres in the room. After reading *The Rainbow Fish* by Marcus Pfister, for example, some children might co-operatively make a tissue-paper fish for the bulletin board above the marina at the Water centre aquarium.

Materials That Encourage Painting

The paint supplies provide their own unique challenge for busy teachers. Brushes, paints, and paper must be of the highest quality and the paints changed regularly since the quality of the work is directly related to the quality of the materials. Parent volunteers or Grade 6 students can be helpful in ensuring this.

How to begin

We recommend introducing this centre with a story such as *The Painter* by Peter Catalanotto or *The Signmaker's Assistant* by Tedd Arnold.

Be sure to spend time talking with the children about how to use the centre. We demonstrated how to set it up, for example, rolling out the oilcloth and clipping on new paper. We also showed how to use the paints carefully, which includes wiping off the brush on the side of the paint pot. At the beginning of the year, we found, routines were more easily established when only primary-colored paints were made available.

We found it best to put out the following materials first:

- different primary-colored paints — red, blue, yellow
- brushes of different sizes
- aprons or old shirts (*not* plastic bags)
- easels or a large table covered with oilcloth or a roll of oilcloth to be used on the floor
- 18 by 24 inch (46 cm by 61 cm) paper of good quality (*not* newsprint)
- sponges and soapy water for cleanup (Adding a little liquid soap to the paints helps with the cleanup.)

It is important to use the classroom bulletin boards to display a painting for *every* child. Doing this may prove challenging because of space in the room, but it is a significant way to contribute to a child's self-esteem — "That's my picture that I made up on the wall!" The bulletin boards dedicated to classroom art could be entitled "Our Art Gallery."

Sustaining interest

We kept this centre alive and interesting by incorporating new painting techniques in addition to the staple paint and paper supplies. At intervals, we added:

- paints of different consistencies (e.g., thick for blobbing, thin for washes)
- paints of different colors (e.g., pastel and primary as well as provisions for mixing in palettes or muffin tins)
- string for string painting
- sponges and "found" materials for printmaking
- squirt bottles for squirt painting
- soap flakes for 3D pictures
- fingerpaint and starch for fingerpainting
- marbles in a box for experimentation and marble painting
- folded paper for symmetry paintings
- Styrofoam plates and pencils to create a template for printmaking

For recipes and instructions for use, see Appendix C: Recipes for Visual Arts Activities.

> ### *Picture Captions*
>
> Before a child begins a painting on a large piece of blank paper, fold back the bottom 10 cm (4 inches) of the paper so that it does not become part of the painting. After the piece is complete, this space will be available for the child who wishes to write a single word, short caption, or full sentence to accompany the image.
>
>
>
> Be sure to add a date to the picture to help show development and progress. At the Visual Arts centre, include a set of children's name cards so that they can attempt to print their own names.

The child's caption can be translated as "This is a princess in a castle."

Materials That Encourage "Make-It" Activities

In our practice, we chose to combine the collage and painting centres as opposed to having separate centres as many of our colleagues choose to do. We wanted the children to use both "make-it" resources and paint to experiment and problem-solve as they created.

As we consistently recommend, we introduced these activities with children's literature. *Lucy's Picture* by Nicola Moon is an excellent book to jump-start interest in collage. In addition, Lois Ehlert has illustrated many children's books that demonstrate the collage technique.

For "make-it" activities, plan to offer the following items:

- glue in small plastic containers with their own lids (It's easy to peel dried glue off the sides of these containers or discard them.)
- other glue materials (e.g., glue sticks, different kinds of tape)
- various weights and sizes of paper kept in cut-down cereal boxes or baskets, one box for each color
- scissors, both right- and left-handed
- a collection of ever changing "found" materials (e.g., sequins, toothpicks, feathers, pipe cleaners, fabric, small boxes, cardboard rolls, cotton balls, and wool of all colors and weights)

We recommend that you encourage children to bring "found" materials from their homes to support their interests and the work of the other centres in the classroom. For example, they might bring in Popsicle sticks to make a ramp for the highway at the Sand centre.

All these materials need to be stored in labelled buckets for easy access and cleanup. We put out only small quantities of available materials to make tidy up more manageable. We also changed the materials in this centre frequently.

Thinking creatively

At the Gathering Time, we gave children an opportunity to show their collage work to the class and share ideas — good artists get ideas and inspiration from other artists. We also explored with the children how they might use various materials, for example, a button as the eye of an animal, the body of a spider, or the centre of a flower. Children need many opportunities to practise thinking creatively.

We gradually introduced new "make-it" techniques, such as two- and three-dimensional work. When it was relevant and purposeful for individuals and small groups of interested children, we provided experience with papier mâché, crushing, scoring, folding, fringing, pleating, and curling. We continually encouraged the children to use these techniques in future work by asking them how they planned to make their giraffe or snowman. "Will it be flat or two or three dimensional?" "What materials will you need for your papier mâché?" "How can you add special features? texture? . . . "

Children enjoy having creative ownership of their work. In our class they did not follow teacher directions for creating the same image, perhaps a ladybug out of pre-cut red and black circles; instead, all the children used the materials in their own creative ways.

Materials That Encourage Modelling Activities

Students may enjoy working with these materials:

cooked playdough	clay
flour and salt	Plasticine

(See Appendix C: Recipes for Visual Arts Activities.) Eventually, all of these materials will be available at the same time.

We found it a good idea to introduce each material in coordination with an activity at one of the other centres in the room. For example, we would introduce Plasticine when examining books by Barbara Reid on a "Favorite Author Table" in the Reading centre. Once the children were familiar with a variety of materials and techniques, we encouraged them to use them for particular projects throughout the year, perhaps to make more farm animals for the farm created in the Sand centre.

These materials need to be stored carefully as they dry out easily. We used air-tight containers, freshening and changing the materials regularly. We preferred to make any of the homemade materials with the children so they could read and follow directions as well as observe and experience changes in properties.

Literacy Activities in the Visual Arts Centre

Reading books and viewing art-related sites on the Internet can help expand literacy development and oral, listening, and reading vocabulary. Books can inspire children to produce beautiful art and Kindergarten teachers can use these texts to help the children explore various artistic techniques, as well as extend their literacy skills.

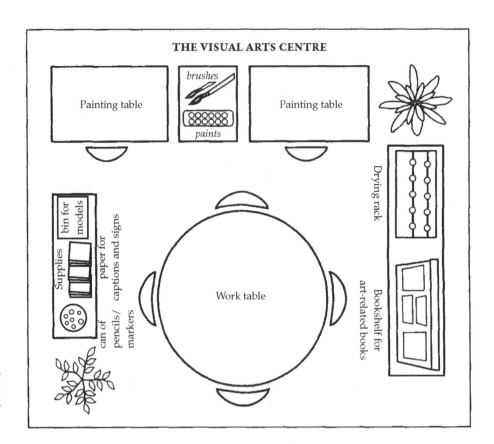

THE VISUAL ARTS CENTRE

Painting table

brushes

paints

Painting table

Drying rack

Supplies

bin for models

paper for captions and signs

can of pencils/ markers

Work table

Bookshelf for art-related books

Art-related books for inspiration and supplies for caption and sign making are all part of a Visual Arts centre that puts an emphasis on literacy.

The following titles have proven to be successful in stimulating literacy extensions in the Visual Arts centre:

- *Market Day: A Story Told with Folk Art* by Lois Ehlert
- *Alphab'Art* by Anne Guery and Olivier Dussutour
- *A Is for Artist: An Alphabet* by Ella Doran, Zoe Miller, and David Goodman

The activities outlined below provide a teacher with many different ways to extend the work of the Visual Arts centre. The choice of extension is dependent upon the interests of the teacher and children. Not all of these extensions would likely take place in the same year.

Playing with color

At the Gathering Time, begin a discussion about color. Read aloud and sing *Pete the Cat: I Love My White Shoes* by Eric Litwin. The children will chuckle as the cat steps on strawberries, blueberries, and then mud, and his sneakers change color. When the author asks, "Was Pete upset?" they love to chant along with the teacher as the words "Goodness No!" are repeated on ensuing pages. The vibrant color background of each changing page helps those children who are just learning to name the colors, while the respective name of each color printed in large, bold font appeals to those who are ready to read.

After the children have had time to manipulate the paints, it is fun to begin experimenting with mixing colors and creating different shades. Read *Mouse Paint* by Ellen Stoll Walsh. The children will delight in viewing and listening as the mouse plays with paints and learns how to create various colors. Explain that artists like to make their own colors by mixing paints.

To help the children role-play artists in a studio, you might provide a few easels, old white shirts collected from parents, and makeshift palettes for combining colors (pieces of wood shaped like an artist's palette or small muffin tins). As the children create new colors, encourage them to add to their descriptive vocabulary by making up different names for their colors, for example, rose red, scarlet red, cherry red, tomato red, and ruby red. You might say, "This shade of red makes me think of a really red tomato. What does it remind you of?" In response, a child might say, "That red is red like a fire truck." To which you might reply, "Great image! Let's call this fire engine red."

You can extend the interest in color in various ways. Collect paint chips from paint stores and allow the children to discover just how many different tints and shades there are. Let the children work with transparencies, or plastic folders that enable them to make new colors through overlaying. Some commercial paddles of different colors and kaleidoscopes are also available to stimulate interest in color. Other motivating books to encourage "talking" about color include *Go Away, Big Green Monster!* by Edward R. Emberley and *Red Leaf, Yellow Leaf* by Lois Ehlert. During large- or small-group discussion times, have a Shared Writing experience where together you create a "color chart." Allow the children to brainstorm the names of new shades and hues. You might further extend this interest by creating a Color board game where the players spin a color dial and proceed to the corresponding colored place on the board. For those children who are beginning readers, you could provide another color spinning dial, which has the names of the colors.

Books About Color

- *Pete the Cat: I Love My White Shoes* by Eric Litwin (illustrated by James Dean)
- *Black and White* by David Macaulay
- *Freight Train* by Donald Crews
- *Purplicious* by Victoria Kann and Elizabeth Kann
- *Pinkalicious* by Victoria Kann and Elizabeth Kann
- *My Many Colored Days* by Dr. Seus
- *Go Away, Big Green Monster!* by Edward R. Emberley
- *Lemons Are Not Red* by Laura Vaccaro Seeger
- *Red Is Best* by Kathy Stinson
- *A Color of His Own* by Leo Lionni
- *Color Farm* by Lois Ehlert

Making a Big Book about color

Lemons Are Not Red by Laura Vaccaro Seeger comes in Big Book format and provides a wonderful experience with color, as the children giggle at the absurdities of "Lemons are not red . . . Lemons are yellow . . . Apples are red" and so on. The predictable pattern of this book makes it an ideal model for the making of a Big Book.

In a small group have each child select a color. Direct the children to use the pattern from *Lemons Are Not Red* to make their own sentences. For example, a child might compose: "Bananas are not orange. Bananas are yellow. Oranges are orange." Invite the children to illustrate their work. Glue each page onto construction paper and then assemble the pages into a book with a bristol board cover, author's page, and publication date.

With so much "talk" about color, it is predictable that more beautiful paintings of colorful patterns, designs, and images will begin to emerge in the children's work.

Rainbows, rainbows, rainbows

A discussion of rainbows is almost sure to emerge with so much inquiry and conversation about color. Almost all children include rainbows in their paintings at one time or another. *Maisy's Rainbow Dream* by Lucy Cousins provides an excellent introduction to rainbows as Maisy and her friends journey through a magnificent, whimsical world of colors. Read *Rainbow Fish A B C* by Marcus Pfister to discover both color and the names of the letters of the alphabet, as the familiar fish swims over, around, and through the letters. Lois Ehlert's *Planting a Rainbow* is another wonderful book that inspires conversation about color, as a little girl and her mother plant a rainbow of flowers in their garden. Marcus Pfister's *Rainbow Fish Opposites* introduces new vocabulary, including *over*, *under*, *big*, and *little*, in a beautifully colorful way.

Using watercolors and water washes

Gather the children in small or large groups to view the watercolor illustrations of *The Lion and the Mouse* by Jerry Pinkney. This beautifully illustrated Caldecott Medal winner for 2010 retells the famous Aesop's fable without words. The children will delight in telling and retelling the story using the illustrations.

Another example of the use of watercolor technique is *Finding Joy* written by Marion Coste and illustrated by Yong Chen. The book tells the poignant story of a baby girl who is born in China and then adopted by a loving family in North America. After reading the book aloud, suggest that interested children water-down both vibrant and pastel colors of paint so that they become faded and pale. These soft versions of colors often motivate the children to paint muted skies, sunsets, and watery scenes. After much experimentation some children often begin to use this technique for backgrounds and washes.

Exploring camouflage

You can help support children's natural interest in animals and their environment. With the children, make a list of animals that have spots, stripes, and color patterns and then encourage the children to use painting and collage techniques to create their own camouflage pictures. You might read Lois Ehlert's *Lots of Spots*, a book that uses collage style to illustrate poems about camouflage. A series of books by Martha E. H. Rustad uses photographs and simple text to help children discover how animals are camouflaged in water, in snow, in the desert, and in the forest. *Why Do Tigers Have Stripes?* by Pamela J. Dell is another good book that has proven successful for young literacy learners.

Eric Carle's tale *Mr. Seahorse* provides an excellent literacy extension for exploring the concept of camouflage. Carle uses transparencies to cleverly disguise and hide sea creatures. It would be fun for the children to use permanent markers on plastic transparencies to simulate their own underwater scenes.

Using a master artist for inspiration: Claude Monet

While it is important not to stifle children's creativity by providing a model or pattern, introducing young children to famous artists and their techniques is valuable. The work of these artists can serve as inspiration for the children's efforts and through it children can learn about art history, as well as the fact that many people turn their passion for art into a career: you might read aloud the moving story *The Painter* by Peter Catalanotto, in which an artist inspires his young son to paint. Here, we are focusing on Claude Monet.

Search the Internet for images of Monet's work and examine copies of famous pieces such as "Monet's Garden" with the children. Talk about the fact that Monet lived long ago in France and find France on a map or globe. If possible, project these images onto a SMART Board so they will be large and clear and the children can see and discuss the colors, subjects, and techniques in Monet's work. Discuss the way that Monet creates his pictures by making many dots and connecting them into an image. Show the children P. I. Maltbie's *Claude Monet: The Painter Who Stopped the Trains*. The book tells the story of how Monet was inspired by his nine-year-old son to experiment with the Impressionist technique. Use the computer to print out other examples of Monet's works and add them to the Visual Arts centre for the children to refer to as they paint. Invite the children to use Monet's dotting technique to create their own paintings and then post them on a bulletin board. Have a small group of children make a large sign that reads something like "Monet's Garden by Room 10."

Consider having the children vote for a favorite painting by Monet. Create a pictorial graph by photographing some of Monet's famous paintings — for example, "Water Lilies" — and during the activity time ask the children to print their names under the painting of their choice. Later, when they have been exposed to many artists and their varied techniques, the children could vote for a favorite artist and orally share the reasons for their vote.

Homework Talk: As a homework assignment, have the children talk to their parents about famous artists, present and past. First, however, be cognizant of the languages spoken at home and ensure that communications sent home are translated or are simple enough for an older sibling to read. Challenge the children to write the names of the artists that their families identify on a piece of paper and bring them to school. You can then compile the names into a class list. Each month throughout the year investigate one of the artists, making your choices based on the children's interest and the easy availability of resources.

Art Gallery Visit: Talking about and investigating various artists might stimulate a visit to a local art gallery or museum. Art galleries often provide postcards or small images of artists' work, and these pieces could be posted at the Visual Arts centre with the names of the artists. Make a matching or Concentration game by collecting duplicates of postcards that show different pieces of artwork (e.g., two Monet water lilies, two Van Gogh sunflowers, two Cézanne peaches).

A B C s of Art: *The ABC's of Art* by Julie Aigner-Clark is a wonderful addition to any Visual Arts centre. It presents 26 famous pictures by different artists and offers important information about these pieces. Some more advanced literacy learners might like to use this format to create their own A B C book of famous artists and their works or contribute to a class book.

With the help of the Internet, this research and experimentation into Monet's work could be repeated with any artist who has a distinct style (e.g., Pablo Picasso, Andy Warhol, or Robert Bateman).

Invitation to an Artists' Tea

Consider inviting parents or caregivers to an Artists' Tea. In a Shared Writing session with a small group, compose a letter to all the parents, inviting them to view the children's artwork and even to purchase their child's work. At the Artists' Tea ensure that the children's work is displayed around the classroom, and consider playing classical music to help set an artistic mood. Prompt the artists to stand beside their work to describe it to their parents and answer questions. Proceeds from art sales could go to a local charity and the purchased items could be given a "red dot sticker" to indicate that they have been sold, just like in a real gallery opening or artist's showing. Enjoying iced tea and cookies is a wonderful way to celebrate after all the work has been shared.

Names and Titles: Point out to the children that artists often sign their name in the corner of the piece and usually give the work a title. Challenge them to do the same with their paintings. Have the children practise a distinctive signature on a whiteboard before they add it to a painting. Printing a title is another opportunity to use and extend their knowledge of sound–symbol relationships.

Further Introductions

To further expose the children to famous artists and their work, we recommend showing them the illustrations in books about the artists at Gathering Time. We used the following books and then put them on an accessible shelf in the Visual Arts centre carefully away from the paint:

- *Henry Matisse: Drawing with Scissors* by Jane O'Connor (illustrated by Jessie Hartland) (Smart About Art series)
- *Matisse: The King of Color* by Laurence Anholt (series)
- *Pablo Picasso: Breaking All the Rules* by True Kelley (Smart About Art series)
- *Claude Monet: Sunshine and Water Lilies* by True Kelley (Smart About Art series)
- *Van Gogh and the Sunflowers* by Laurence Anholt (series)
- *Vincent van Gogh: Sunflowers and Swirly Stars* by Jane Holub (Smart About Art series)
- *Edward Degas: Paintings That Dance* by Maryann Cocca-Leffler
- *Pierre-Auguste Renoir: Paintings That Smile* by True Kelley (Smart About Art series)

Eric Hill's black-outlined images

Eric Hill is a favorite author among Kindergarten classes, and his simple, colorful illustrations are characterized by a thick black outline around the images. Select several of his Spot books from the school library/resource centre and share them with the children. These books might be added to a Favorite Author Table or collected in a labelled bin — "Eric Hill Spot Books" — so that the children can refer to them.

Point out Hill's outlining technique and then provide each child with a large piece of paper and a thick black marker to create images. These images can later be colored in with thick markers or shaded with crayons. Teach the children to take the paper off a few crayons and then turn them on their side for a shading technique. Save these crayons for future use at the Visual Arts centre.

It might be meaningful to have the children use this outlining technique to make large, self-portraits. They could accompany these pieces by good-sized speech bubbles showing print that helps introduce them. The pieces could be posted outside the classroom at the beginning of the year (the sample text below appears in standard English).

> *I am Charlie. I am in Senior Kindergarten.*
> *I am in Room 102.*
> *I am Janetta. I live with my Grandma.*
> *Hi! I am Omar.*

As a follow-up, more advanced literacy learners could make their own book of black-outlined illustrations accompanied by captions like these:

Mi Fmlee	for "My Family"
s is mi b str	for "This is my baby sister."
s is mi bg br	for "This is my big brother."

Photo shots

Many children's books include black-and-white or color photographs. Read Tana Hoban's *Look Again!* to the children and then discuss why an author or illustrator might like to use photographs, as opposed to drawings, collage, or paintings. (Ideas include achieving a realistic effect and true colours, and being able to show expressions on people's faces.) Talk to the children about the difference between a snapshot that might catch people smiling, posing, and looking at the camera and an artistic photograph that may not include people. Discuss how a photo can be taken on an angle or from above, from close up or far away. Discuss, too, how the photographer needs to consider what is in the background before taking a photo. All this teaching could be done easily if you take a variety of photos from different vantage points — for example, from above and below — and present them to the children on a SMART Board so they could be examined and discussed.

Provide each child with an opportunity to apply this learning: invite class members to take a series of digital pictures in the classroom. If digital cameras are not available, have the children use disposable cameras. This photography activity works well in pairs or with children from a higher grade.

Load the children's work onto the computer to examine and have the children select their most effective piece. Invite them to create a short piece of writing, even poetry, to accompany this photograph. These pieces could even be assembled into a class book or a published book with the aid of an Internet photography site. The title could be "All About Kindergarten" and the book could feature photographic images of the children working at various classroom centres, for example, Water centre, Home/Dramatic Play centre, and Reading centre.

Eric Carle and tissue paper collage

With simple, repetitive patterns in many of his books, Eric Carle is an effective author to feature at the Favorite Author Table; his work is also a popular choice for Big Book read-alouds. Beyond that, you can extend learning about him to the Visual Arts centre.

At a Gathering Time, introduce the children to Eric Carle, illustrator, by examining the pictures in his books and looking at his website: www.ericcarle.com. You might work with a SMART Board or ask the teacher who runs a computer lab to introduce the children to this website in the lab.

On his site, Carle effectively demonstrates and describes his inspirations and artistic technique. He begins his artistic process by creating collage paper. He paints large pieces of white tissue paper and uses many bright colors to make lines, circles, dots, waves, and squiggles — the result is many vibrant and interesting papers. When the papers are dry, Carle uses them to cut and paste his collage pictures of animals, nature, and, of course, the sun. The results are impressive and will motivate children to create their own pieces, "just like Eric Carle," at the Visual Arts centre. Instead of painting white tissue paper, they could use commercial tissue paper, as Carle did when he published his first book.

Barbara Reid and Plasticine art

Present Barbara Reid's award-winning work to the children. You might read aloud *Have You Seen Birds?* and *The Party*. Discuss Reid's unique technique and then log on to her website: www.barbarareid.com. Watch the three-part video in which Reid demonstrates and describes her Plasticine art technique. Gather many vibrant colors of Plasticine or playdough (see recipe in Appendix C: Recipes for Visual Arts Activities), individual plywood boards, and many texturing tools including toothpicks, tongue depressors, combs, pencils, and Lego pieces. Invite the children to use their imaginations to make individual illustrations using a technique much like Barbara Reid's.

When the illustrations are complete, take full-frame, close-up photographs to preserve the work. Depending on their writing level, challenge the children to write a word, caption, sentence, or several sentences to create a simple story to accompany their picture. These photos and writing pieces will compile beautifully into a class book titled "Just Like Barbara Reid."

Lauren Child and magazine clip art

Lauren Child is the author and illustrator of a series of books about the adventures of a little girl named Lola and her big brother, Charlie. These simple books deal with real-life situations that appeal to the young reader's sense of humor. Some of the text is written in oversized font which makes the books effective for developing readers. The illustrations in Lauren Child's books are drawings that include one item that looks different than the rest — this feature has been cut out of a magazine or newspaper so it looks realistic in comparison to the rest of the drawing.

Challenge the children to produce a Lauren Child–inspired piece of art. Search through children's magazines for appropriate images such as animals, vehicles, furniture, flowers, and plants. Confer with the children to select an image; then, discuss its position on the page and what to draw around it. The children could use markers, pencils, crayons, or even chalk or pastels to complete these illustrations. The completed pieces will make an effective bulletin board to share with the school. Have a small group print a title for the board, perhaps "Magazine Clip Art."

Using the Squiggle or the Dot

Read the children the book *The Squiggle* by Carole Lexa Schaefer. This creative book presents the same piece of string on each page and each time it is transformed into a different image — for example, a skipping rope, fireworks, the

Children's pieces could be posted on a bulletin board to share with the entire school or compiled into a class book titled "Becoming Eric Carle." You may want to have the children complete their exciting projects in conjunction with an older class or Reading Buddy class.

moon. Provide the children with a piece of string and challenge them to use it to inspire an illustration. These pieces could be compiled into a class book titled "Our Squiggles."

Another book that provides a similar experience is *The Dot* by Peter H. Reynolds. A young learner is reluctant to paint, but the teacher encourages the child to make a mark or a dot. The images of large, small, and composite dots make the child proud and happy to sign his name to his work. Have the children create their own dot pictures from the inspiration in this book.

Framing Pictures

Here is one way to create a more elaborate picture frame for each child.

1. Take a large piece of white bristol board and use pencil to draw a large *X* in the centre of the paper. Each end of the *X* should be about 10 cm (4 inches) from the corner of the paper.
2. Cut the *X* and gently fold out each of the four pieces.
3. Staple or pin the four corners of paper up on the wall
4. Bend back the four triangular pieces of the frame and pin them to the wall.

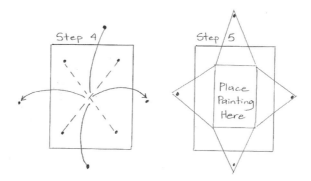

5. Place the child's painting within the frame. Enjoy!

Such paintings can be easily removed and sent home to share with family when it's time to replace them with other masterpieces. As an alternative, add paintings to the frame, on top of one another, and send the collection home at the end of the year.

Creating an Environment for Success in the Visual Arts Centre

The following section is presented in terms of questions that the reflective practitioner is encouraged to ask about the classroom's Visual Arts centre. The answers reflect what we have found to be best practices.

1. How do I ensure that the materials are accessible and available on a regular basis?

- The Visual Arts centre needs to be open during every Literacy and the Arts activity time, not just on one particular afternoon each week.

- Encourage the children to use visual arts materials to respond to other areas of the curriculum, such as a story, a trip, an experience from home, an extension of work at one of the other centres. (For example, the children might use baskets from the Visual Arts centre to make cages for the animals at a zoo they created in the Sand centre.)

2. How do I ensure that I have samples of work to demonstrate the progress of the children over time?

- Have the children date-stamp all work samples.
- Place selected samples of work for all children in a portfolio made from two pieces of bristol board stapled together.

3. How can I help parents understand the importance of their responses to their children's work?

- Send home regular newsletters or emails with suggestions of positive, constructive responses parents can offer their children. (Examples: "Tell me about your picture." "I love the way you used so many colors." "It's very clever the way you have made Daddy bigger than you.")
- Post signs at the centre, highlighting the learning and its importance.
- At parent–teacher conferences, regularly use samples of work to discuss the learning that is taking place.

4. How do I help all of the children realize that their work is valued and worthwhile?

- Be sure to respond positively to the efforts of all the children.
- Take the time to help the children extend their work. Say, for example, "I really like how you used . . . ," "I wonder how you might . . . ?"
- Accept and celebrate all approximations while encouraging effort and developmental growth.
- Resist any temptation to demand that all children make the same product. In other words, don't ask all the children to copy a model of a snowman you have created.
- Share the work with the whole group at celebration time.
- Point out creative efforts, ideas, and techniques.
- Ask the children to describe the process they used.
- Send home work that elicits parental comments. For example, you could provide a comments page for responses to a collaborative class book.

5. How do I ensure that I have time to help children extend their learning, develop their understandings, skills, and attitudes, and consolidate their skills?

- Share the responsibility for room maintenance with the children. For example, have the children wash the paintbrushes, wash the glue brushes, wipe paint spills, and clip more paper onto the paint easels.
- Require the children to check in with you when they have completed their work so you can provide a comment or offer a challenge.
- Encourage the children to go to their peers for help and solutions.
- Model by asking, "How do you think you might find out the answer to your question?"

6. How do I ensure that the children feel ownership of and responsibility for their work?

- Have the children determine what they want to make, paint, or create..
- Encourage the children to make their own decisions about what artistic method they will use.
- Encourage the children to use this centre to respond to ideas generated in the other centres (e.g., Sand, Water, Construction).
- Invite the children to evaluate their own work and the work of others.

Mileposts to Help Guide Teacher Observations of Children Engaged in Visual Arts

When making observations, be sure to remember the developmental nature of children's learning. Skills, knowledge, and interests are not acquired in a lock-step, linear, sequential manner. Children move back and forth on the continuum according to their experiences, circumstances, and materials. The mileposts outlined below and others listed in the book are offered merely as a guide — they are not intended to be prescriptive or rigid. It is not expected that all children will demonstrate all of these learnings in the order they are presented. Teachers who listen to and watch their children closely will undoubtedly observe other behavior and learning.

How children show interest in visual arts

Children show interest by choosing to use art materials to express their ideas, for example, their response to a story. They might use all the materials available — paints, modelling materials, "found" materials, and more — and they use the materials with confidence. They try different techniques that have been introduced, perhaps sponge-painting to add texture to a picture. They experiment with new ideas. They also persevere and complete projects.

Literacy skills that children demonstrate

- Children listen to other children describe their work and offer increasingly appropriate and encouraging comments.
- They talk about their own work, offering increasingly descriptive explanations.
- They answer peers' questions with increasing confidence and more descriptive explanation.
- They refer increasingly to books and other resource materials for ideas for their work.
- They retell with increasing accuracy the steps they took to produce their work.
- Children relate what they have done to other pieces of work. For example, a child might say, "I used watery paint like in the cover of the Eric Carle books to make a background for my picture of my dog."
- Children reflect on what they have accomplished and offer some insights on what they might do on their next piece of work. A child might say, "I want to make a boat that floats for the Water centre and see how many paper clips it will hold before it sinks. I am going to make a clay one and a playdough one to see which works the best."

- Children add words or short captions to their work, for example, *mi mom* ("My Mom").
- Children add short sentences with increasingly accurate print to the work. They say, for example, *Ths is a graf I sa at the zoo.*

Painting-related skills that children demonstrate

Children have different ways of using the paintbrush, among them the following:

- using their whole fist or their thumb and finger
- holding the end or middle of the brush
- moving between the pot of paint and paper in one movement with no drips
- wiping the excess paint off the brush

Children show different ways of using paint, including the following.

- They dab paint on the paper using one color or scrub the brush over one area with one color.

- They experiment with several colors, joining the dabs into curved and straight lines using one or several colors.

- They make curved lines into circles and ovals, sometimes filling them in.
- They take circles and ovals and lines and begin to make symbols, such as the sun, letters, and numerals.
- They take circles and ovals and begin to make symbols of body images.

- They add more lines, dots, and dabs to make a more detailed person, perhaps one with fingers, clothes, and hair.

- They show houses or apartments that enclose people.
- They add recognizable symbols of other familiar objects in the environment, for example, trees and flowers.
- They use other media and found materials, for example, glitter and construction paper.

- They adopt a baseline and a skyline.

- They show profiles, perspective, and relative size.

The Visual Arts centre contributes to small muscle development and eye-hand coordination which are critical to the later work in upper grades with printing and cursive writing.

How children control materials in "make-it" activities

Children might control the materials in any of the following ways:

- applying glue with fingers, glue brushes, or sticks
- using alternative methods to attach materials, such as tape, stapler, glue stick
- using an appropriate amount of glue with control
- tearing materials
- cutting materials with an adult holding the material
- cutting independently with some control
- cutting with increasing control

How children use "found" materials

Children might use "found" materials in any of the following ways:

- randomly choosing and gluing "found" materials together
- making patterns or designs
- selecting materials for a specific purpose, for example, feathers for a box sculpture bird; sequins for a sparkly coat
- working on projects over time, for example, making a papier mâché dinosaur

How children use modelling materials

Children might work with modelling materials in any of the following ways:

- using hands and fingers to manipulate the materials

- using other tools to manipulate the materials, for example, blunt plastic cutlery
- experimenting with different textures, for example, scratching, scoring
- rolling the materials into long rolls or balls to create 2D or 3D symbols, such as a snowman or the sun
- using other materials to create details, for example, wool for hair; sequins for buttons
- creating sculptures, such as soap carvings, by using hands and tools to carve the material

The Visual Arts centre is an area of the classroom where children can express their ideas and feelings about a variety of topics. Here they paint, cut and paste, sculpt, and learn to use various artistic techniques.

But as we did with other classroom centres, we came to see how this centre could be successfully infused with literacy. We created an ebb and flow between large- and small-group discussions at this critical centre, the Visual Arts. Children and teachers were able to brainstorm, share relevant literature and resources, and make plans for exciting visual arts experiences. These experiences, we recognized, contributed to the children's literacy knowledge and development.

6

The Home/Dramatic Play Centre

The Home/Dramatic Play centre is a place where children can explore their world and make sense of experiences, relationships, feelings, and everyday events. It has always been a popular choice for young children. They love to dramatize familiar roles. By exploring familiar and imaginary roles, children gain a deeper understanding of everyday experiences. They have many opportunities to sort out their actions and reactions and to rehearse their responses to past and upcoming events. As children role-play, they learn to take risks in familiar supportive settings, and in doing so, build their self-confidence and self-esteem. The Home/Dramatic Play centre is of critical importance in the emotional, social, and intellectual growth of each young child.

In addition to the creative and social benefits, the Home/Dramatic Play centre provides many natural and meaningful opportunities for children to develop literacy skills. The centre can be transformed from the Home centre into many other dramatic settings, including a bank, hairdresser, or shoe store. The Home/Dramatic Play centre, with its many possible extensions, introduces oral and written language in exciting and relevant ways (e.g., a grocery list in the home, environmental print found at a bank, magazines in an airplane, or For Sale signs in a real-estate office). The children have many authentic reasons to speak, listen, read, write, view, and represent.

Children use their imaginations and creativity to communicate and express themselves when role-playing in this centre. They truly live the experience.

Materials That Encourage Literacy Learning in the Home/Dramatic Play Centre

We introduced this language-promoting centre by reading aloud a story such as *The Family Book* by Todd Parr. This book talks about different families and different family members. As the year progressed, we often read additional books that highlighted different family structures. These ones are recommended:

- *Families Are Different* by Nina Pelligrini
- *Raising You Alone* by Warren Hanson
- *Oh the Things Mommies Do!: What Could Be Better Than Having Two?* by Crystal Tompkins (illustrated by Lindsey Evans)
- *Who's in a Family?* by Robert Skutch (illustrated by Laura Nienhaus)

If these books are unavailable to you, ask your teacher-librarian for suitable materials.

Three special considerations

After the first read-aloud, we took the children on a walk through the centre and introduced them to the routines and expectations. The centre we set up reflected the following three considerations.

1. When selecting materials, we were careful to include bias-free materials that were inclusive of race, age, gender, and culture, and representative of a variety of family structures. For example, in addition to picture books, we chose dolls that represented different races (e.g., Asian, white, and black), different ages (babies and toddlers), and different genders (male and female). We also provided food labels, store flyers, and restaurant menus featuring food from different cultures (e.g., Chinese, Italian, French, Indian, and Japanese).
2. We ensured that the materials and props represented the broader community and global village. One good example was the inclusion of lengths of cloth for use as skirts, shawls, and saris, as well as tablecloths and baby blankets. The children could then create their own costumes as they determined necessary.
3. Issues of safety and hygiene were also addressed: to help prevent the spread of head lice we did not provide any head coverings unless they were made of easily washed plastic or disposable paper.

Initially, we limited the materials to ensure a successful tidy-up.

Necessary elements

Here are some necessary materials that are effective in fostering literacy development in the Home centre:

Beyond materials that specifically apply to this centre, familiar materials, such as a doctor's bag or cash register, could be stored in a bin for spontaneous use when the Home centre is transformed into something else.

- child-sized furniture, such as a stove, refrigerator, small table, and chairs
- accessories found in the home — real items where possible — for example, telephone, iron, dishes
- baby and toddler dolls representing different ages, sexes, and races (We recommend providing one doll less than the number of children who could use the centre to increase the opportunities for sharing and negotiation.)
- different sizes of clothes to fit the dolls (We provided inclusive or multi-purpose clothing of different sizes with different fasteners to provide natural opportunities for the children to develop their small muscle coordination and control.)
- real accessories for the dolls, such as baby bottles, bibs, rattles, strollers, and cribs
- child-sized clothing for dress-up

We encouraged the children to bring other accessories for dolls from home to add to the collection.

- other real accessories, such as eyeglasses, jewellery, wallets, cell phones
- adaptable items for dress-up (e.g., pieces of cloth, scarves)
- plastic models of food
- adaptable items to make their own models of food (e.g., playdough for spaghetti)
- cooking utensils and dishes that represent a variety of cultures (e.g., woks, chopsticks, pasta bowls)
- environmental print, such as that found on food packages
- other print materials to extend the role-play (e.g., cheques, books, menus, message board, magnetic letters)

We were careful to include reading materials at a variety of reading levels and in the different home languages of the children.

- reading materials, such as magazines, children's literature (narrative, expository, poetry, non-fiction, and fiction), telephone books, recipe books, flyers, newspapers, and computer reading programs, such as *A to Z Reading*

Books for the Home Centre

The following reading materials help children validate their own family structures. They also introduce the children to a range of family structures that may be different from their own.

- *Are You My Mother?* by P. D. Eastman
- *Dinosaurs Divorce: A Guide for Changing Families* by Laurene Krasny Brown and Marc Brown
- *Homes: What Living Things Need* by Vic Parker
- *Homes of Living Things* by Bobbie Kalman
- *Houses and Homes* by Ann Morris (illustrated by Ken Heyman)
- *Hug* by Jez Alborough
- *I Love You Through and Through* by Bernadette Rossetti-Shustak and Caroline Jayne Church
- *In Our House* by Anne F. Rockwell
- *Molly's Family* by Nancy Garden
- *My New Family: A Look at Adoption* by Pat Thomas and Lesley Harker
- *The Daddy Book* by Todd Parr
- *The Family Book* by Todd Parr
- *The Mommy Book* by Todd Parr
- *We Belong Together* by Todd Parr
- *What Daddies Do Best* by Laura Numeroff (illustrated by Lynn Munsinger)
- *What Grandmas Do Best* by Laura Numeroff (illustrated by Lynn Munsinger)
- *What Mommies Do Best* by Laura Numeroff (illustrated by Lynn Munsinger)

Literacy Activities in the Home Centre

We always began the year with the Home/Dramatic Play centre set up as a home with limited materials. As the children became more familiar with this centre, we added materials, for example, model vegetables and fruits, baking pans, spatulas, and serving spoons. We found it important to follow the interests and lead of the children when we were deciding what additional materials might enhance the children's literacy learning. Extensions added by us were rarely as successful as those that occurred as a natural result of the children's dramatic play.

There are many small- and large-group activities that can extend or build upon the literacy learning in the Home centre. Besides the obvious and natural exposure to print from labelling drawers, listing addresses, making shopping lists, and using message pads, there are many wonderful opportunities to introduce literacy in meaningful ways.

Parts of a house

If you read aloud *In Our House* by Anne Rockwell, you can then talk with the children about the various parts of a house. This book explores a house where a family of bears lives. As they go about their busy day, the bears introduce the reader to every room in their house and describe all the activities in each room. With the class, create a large labelled diagram showing roof, windows, walls, door, and so on, and then post it in the Home centre. Some children may want to complete their own diagrams by drawing an image of a house and labelling it with the help of the large group's chart.

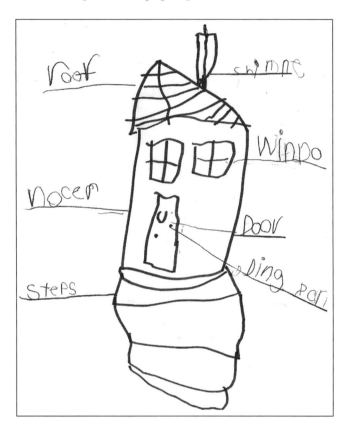

Here, a child has drawn and labelled a house exterior.

At another time reread *In Our House* and ask the children to notice any jobs that happen in the various rooms of the house. After the reading, list all the chores that the children are able to recollect from the book. Brainstorm other chores that need to be done in a home, for example, cooking, cleaning, washing clothes, ironing, washing dishes, taking out garbage, and mowing the lawn. Make a word web of the suggested chores in a Shared Writing experience. (See Appendix A: Ways to Record Ideas.)

Kinds of homes

After a neighborhood walk, have a Shared Writing session to create a word web displaying different kinds of homes (e.g., apartments, houses, bungalows, duplexes, and retirement home). Invite the children to add illustrations or magazine pictures to the web. Some more advanced literacy learners might develop their own word webs of kinds of homes in their drawing and writing book.

The initial discussion might lead into consideration of animal homes (e.g., chicken coop, barn, pigsty, shell, and nest). If so, the class could create a word web of different animal homes or games with pictures and initial consonants or words (see Appendix B: Games). You might make a lift-the-flap book with children's drawings of animal homes and words. *A House for Hermit Crab* by Eric Carle can support this focus on animal homes.

Family members

Cross-Centre Connections

Encourage children at the Drawing/Writing centre to draw pictures of their family members. The children could label these illustrations with initial consonants or full words. Later, collate these family representations into an "Our Families" class book and place the book in the Reading centre.

Read aloud Nick Butterworth's series that describes all the special abilities and fine qualities of various family members (*My Mom Is Excellent, My Dad Is Awesome, My Grandma Is Wonderful*, and *My Grandpa Is Amazing*). Talk with the children about the members of their own family (e.g., sister, mother, grandfather, and aunt) and list the members in a chart. During a read-aloud time, consider reading the wonderful *Celebrating Families* by Rosmarie Hausherr. This book recognizes many kinds of families, including single-parent, two-parent, multiracial, and interracial. Many of the above-mentioned books about family could be placed in the Home centre for future reference, along with small, racially representative models of various family members, perhaps made of wood or plastic. At the centre, children may role-play based on books read to them, for example, acting out a family's adoption of a baby.

Environmental print in the home

The addition of food packages to the Home centre often stimulates an interest in print. Encourage the children to contribute any items that have labels attached, for example, cereal boxes, soup cans, and cookie boxes. Ask the children to categorize these foods and place them in labelled bins or shelves in the Home centre. Many informal and group discussions will take place, as the children enjoy role-playing with these items.

To further extend the play, add other models of foods, maybe fruits and vegetables, and place them in labelled containers with either pictures or printed text. During a Shared Writing session, you might sort these foods into breakfast, lunch, dinner, and snack foods and record the decisions. You can further build on this interest by reading *Today Is Monday* by Eric Carle at a read-aloud time. The book is cleverly presented in song format, featuring foods for each day of the week. The children might be interested in identifying their favorite food (with a picture or letter or printed word) on a chart next to their name.

All about babies

Invite the children to bring copies of their baby photographs to school. After looking at the photographs and talking about them, display them on a bulletin board at the children's eye level; then, make a Concentration game with the name of the Kindergartner and the appropriate baby photo. (See Appendix B: Games.)

The dolls in the Home centre often stimulate further interest in babies. To extend this interest and provide rich literacy experiences, you might read aloud *Ten Little Fingers and Ten Little Toes* by Mem Fox. This simple text emphasizes that, although we are different in many ways, we are also much the same. Children enjoy chiming in with the repetitive, rhythmic parts of the text during Shared Reading sessions.

After reading the Mem Fox book, consider expanding the interest in mothers and babies by reading *Does a Kangaroo Have a Mother, Too?* by Eric Carle. This beautifully illustrated text introduces children to the names of many animals and

A child shows a baby and a mother animal.

Tidying Up

"The dolls are all over the floor."

At the end of an activity period, a child might report on the tidy up at the Home/Dramatic Play centre.

The teacher would then likely ask the group, "Would the people who were working at that centre please go back and finish the tidy up? Could someone show them where to put the dolls? Many thanks."

Children are often sent to check on the status of the tidy up in the various centres. If the tidy up is not yet done or has not been done correctly, they may be asked to help with the tidy up or to return to the centre where they worked to finish it.

their babies. Once the children are familiar with the oral vocabulary, you can develop literacy further by printing the names of each baby and mother on a T-chart. At the Drawing/Writing centre, some children may extend their interest by creating booklets using repetitive words and cloze format:

A baby _____ is called a _____.
A baby *kangaroo* is called a *joey*.

These child-made books become favorites to read in the Reading centre with the children taking turns being the teacher!

Caring for baby

Since many children have babies at home or are familiar with a neighbor's newborn, they have first-hand knowledge of how families care for babies. Brainstorm all the items that are necessary in caring for a baby, such as a crib, stroller, and highchair. In a Shared Writing experience, create a chart with words and pictures cut out from baby magazines.

To develop active listening skills, play What Is in the Baby's Diaper Bag?, a large-group, circle game. The teacher starts the game by saying, "Mommy had a diaper in the baby's diaper bag." A child repeats the pattern and adds another item. "Mommy had a diaper and a rattle in the baby's diaper bag." Each subsequent child in the circle repeats the names of the items already identified and adds another item, for example, a pacifier, a bottle, or a blanket. Encourage the children to bring such real items from home where possible and add them to the Home centre for the children to use and talk about during their play there.

Reading to baby

Collect baby board books by encouraging the children to bring in baby books from home that they would like to share with the class. Sometimes if the family speaks another first language, the books will not be in English — these too make marvellous additions to the Home centre.

If possible, try to obtain books from Karen Katz's wonderful series of board books for babies. Titles include *Where Is Baby's Belly Button?*, *Counting Kisses: A Kiss and Read Book*, *Where Is Baby's Mommy?*, *Grandpa and Me*, and *Grandma and Me*. The text is always simple and repetitive, and these books, most presented in a lift-the-flap format, lend themselves well to children reading them in role to baby dolls in the Home centre. After hearing the books being read aloud at a large-group time, the children are sure to meet with success in memory-reading these texts to the dolls.

Lullabies for baby

Many cultures sing lullabies to comfort babies. At a singing session, ask the children to share lullabies they know. Print a popular lullaby such as "Twinkle, Twinkle, Little Star" or "Are You Sleeping?" ("Frère Jacques") on large chart paper and point to the words as you sing it with the children. After a few days and repeated singing, cover the last word in each line and ask the children to sing the song filling in the missing words. This is one approach to cloze procedure. Make the lullaby chart available for the children to read and sing while at the Home centre. The children will enjoy reading and singing the song to the dolls.

In a Shared Writing session, create a letter to parents about lullabies. Be sure to write in large font on chart paper or equivalent. Ask the parents to send in the lyrics of a lullaby they like to sing in their home, and invite them to visit the

Kindergarten to sing the lullaby to the children. Once the class has composed the large version, type out the letter on letter-size paper and give each child a copy to bring home. Children might decide to sign their names and add drawings.

Later, collate the lullabies that families submit into a class book. Ask interested children to illustrate the pages. Read aloud other texts that focus on familiar lullabies and nursery rhymes, too. After the children become familiar with rhymes recorded on a large chart, cut each line into a strip and invite some children to reconstruct the rhymes using all the strips.

This Home centre setup includes theme-related books and supplies for home-related writing.

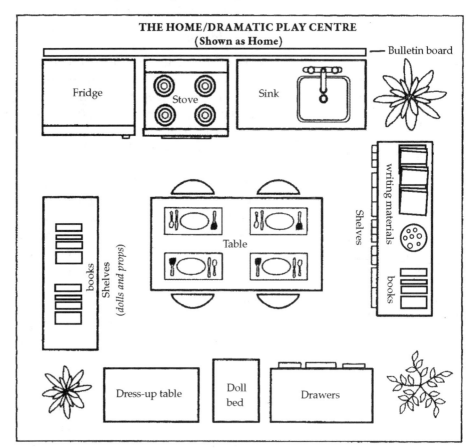

Transforming the Home Centre into Other Dramatic Play Settings

The Home/Dramatic Play centre facilitates the development of many listening, reading, writing, and oral language skills. All the learning at the Home centre can be enriched, supported, and extended by transforming the centre into various different settings, including familiar places. Changing the home to a store, a veterinarian's office, or a travel agency, for example, can provide many opportunities for children to acquire and use new vocabulary, enact new roles, and gain exposure to print in meaningful ways.

Below a number of possible literacy experiences are outlined. Not all would be implemented in one school year, but all have proven to be extremely successful in Kindergarten classrooms. In transforming the Home centre, we sometimes found it necessary to remove some pieces of the furniture, while at other times, it was enough simply to cover some furniture with pieces of cloth. For example, a campsite would not require any furniture, while a vet's office could make good use of a refrigerator.

In order to support literacy development, you will need to visit the centre, interact with the children, and observe them carefully. Be sure to note when interest in a different dramatic setting is waning — we often re-established the Home centre when that occurred. Re-establishing the Home centre will provide the children with additional time to role-play and clarify their personal role in the family. As always, follow the lead and interests of your students.

Fairy-tale extensions

After hearing a favorite story such as "Three Billy Goats Gruff" at a large-group time, the children often spontaneously transformed the Home centre into a setting where they could act out portions of the story. They might negotiate use of the big blocks or tables to change the shape of the centre, later returning the blocks to the closed Construction centre at the end of the activity period. In addition to the props we suggested (e.g., blocks or planks for the bridge, large pieces of fabric to represent the meadow, and drums to represent the hooves of the goats on the bridge), children typically brought props from home. In our experience, every time the children use props at this centre, they improvise, creating unique versions of old and familiar stories.

Other stories and related props that motivate dramatic play include these:

- "Little Red Riding Hood" (red cape, wolf costume, picnic basket)
- "Little Red Hen" (animal hats, burlap for flour)
- "The Three Little Pigs" (pig noses, wolf costume, bricks, sticks, straw)
- "Cinderella" (plastic slipper, dresses, aprons, broom, crowns, wand)

Storytelling activities can also be effectively done on a felt board. When selecting stories, we looked for a simple plot line, a limited number of characters, and to make our task easier, the availability of commercial felt cut-outs. Felt cut-outs encourage the children to use language from the story to retell the events at the beginning, middle, and end.

Be sure to provide various versions of these stories at the centre for the children to discuss, compare, retell, and enjoy (see the box below). Including books that continue the traditional fairy tale or that present a fractured version of the plot will help extend the story experience. For example, *A Chair for Baby Bear* by Kaye Umansky is a delightful story that explains what happens after Goldilocks runs away.

Familiar Stories: Alternative Versions

For "The Three Little Pigs"

The Three Little Pigs by Paul Galdone
The True Story of the 3 Little Pigs by Jon Scieszka (illustrated by Lane Smith)
The Three Little Pigs: An Architectural Tale by Steve Guarnaccia
Ziggy Piggy and the Three Little Pigs by Frank Asch

For "Goldilocks and the Three Bears"

Goldilocks and the Three Bears by James Marshall
Goldilocks and the Three Bears by Caralyn Buehner (illustrated by Mark
    Buehner) *Tackylocks and The Three Bears* by Helen Lester
A Chair for Baby Bear by Kaye Umansky
Baby Bear's Chairs by Jane Yolen (illustrated by Melissa Sweet)
Somebody and the Three Blairs by Marilyn Tolhurst (illustrated by Simone
    Abel)

For "Cinderella"

Cinderella by Marcia Brown (a traditional version to be read first)
Cinder-Elly by Frances Minters (illustrated by G. Brian Karas)
Yeh-Shen: A Cinderella Story from China by Ai-Ling Louie
Mufaro's Beautiful Daughters: An African Tale by John Steptoe
The Korean Cinderella by Shirley Climo (illustrated by Ruth Heller)
The Egyptian Cinderella by Shirley Climo (illustrated by Ruth Heller)
Prince Cinders by Babette Cole

You may want to have the children vote orally, in pictorial form or print, about which story version they liked the best. (Appendix A: Ways to Record Ideas provides instructions on how to make a voting sheet.)

Travel agency

The children in our teaching communities come from many different parts of the world and are interested in learning about foreign lands — establishing a travel agency setting is one way to address this. *Gifts* by Jo Ellen Bogart (illustrated by Barbara Reid) is a wonderful introduction to a few countries, as a grandmother travels around the world and gathers souvenir gifts for her granddaughter. *Miss Rumphius* by Barbara Cooney is another recommended fiction title. At read-aloud time, also read simple non-fiction books about countries and places to stimulate discussion.

Before a read-aloud session, establish prior knowledge by asking the children to identify where they or their parents were born, perhaps Canada, China, or the Philippines. Make a list of these places with a small or large group. Take the opportunity to point out initial consonants, spacing, and so on during the Shared Writing experience. Use the large chart created to transform the Home centre into a travel agency.

Children working at the Visual Arts centre can contribute to the creation of a travel agency. Challenge some of the children to paint pictures that represent places such as mountains, oceans, and the CN Tower, and post the art in the new travel agency. By visiting a local travel agency, you should be able to collect related literacy items, including travel brochures, airplane tickets, itinerary sheets, and posters from around the world. Include these at the travel agency.

Provide a template for a passport that children can show as they board the plane for a trip. Children could bring in small photos of themselves from home. Be sure, too, to include paper and pencils to encourage the children to create plane tickets and information about the dates and times of the holidays. (See the sample on the next page.)

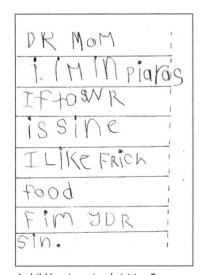

A child has imagined visiting France and filled in a simple postcard template. The message home is shown: *Dear Mom, I am in Paris. Eiffel Tower is shiny. I like French food. From your son.*

Airplane Ticket

Name CHARLIE

Date JAN, 28, 2011.

Time 3:00.PM.

Destination TAMPA

Seat Number 883

The airplane ticket is an example of an easily prepared template that students can readily use in their dramatic play. The child has clearly communicated his travel intentions.

Airplane: As an extension, several chairs could be arranged in rows with a middle aisle and the travel agency could be changed into an airplane. Each chair could be labelled with a row and seat number, and given an assigned ticket. A small rolling cart could be filled with empty pop cans or bottles, as well as plastic food for the flight attendants to serve to the passengers.

Pizza parlor/Restaurant

Read *Hi! Pizza Man* by Virginia Walter or *Pete's a Pizza* by William Steig to the large group and use the text to create a chart listing various pizza toppings, such as pepperoni, pineapple, cheese, tomatoes, and peppers.

For the centre, use colored felt to cut out topping items and sort them into various labelled baskets; make them available for the children to make their own pizzas. Collect cooking items such as aluminum pizza pans, spatulas, plastic pizza cutters, oven mitts, and paper chef hats. Be sure to label the place for each item with pictures or words to ensure an organized tidy-up. You might cover the table with a red-and-white checkered cloth to give the feel of a real pizzeria — local dollar stores are often good sources for these resources. Have the children paint large pictures of pizzas and cut them out to display on the bulletin boards in the centre. Visit your favorite local pizza take-out restaurant and ask for several unused pizza boxes, menus, and flyers. Obtaining these items will add to the authenticity of the restaurant.

Involve the children in developing the print resources required for a restaurant. During a shared modelled writing experience, create a poster indicating the daily specials and restaurant hours. Be sure to provide pencils and small pads of paper so that the children, in role as waiters, can record customers' orders. These order pads could show a combination of pictures and words, for example, different sizes of wedges to represent different pizza sizes. Plan to develop them with a small group of children in a Shared Writing session. Finally, provide the children with pieces of blank chart or painting paper, folded in thirds, so that they can create their own pizza recipes and menus.

A child in role as waiter said, "A large pepperoni and a medium cheese cost lots of money so I made lots of dollars."

Have the children brainstorm other kinds of restaurants and alter and use many of these ideas to transform the centre into a different restaurant, such as a traditional Chinese restaurant equipped with chopsticks, rice bowls, and bamboo placemats.

Shoe store

Reading *Shoes, Shoes, Shoes* by Ann Morris or *Whose Shoes?* by Anna Grossnickle Hines is a good way to introduce a shoe-store setting. At a subsequent Shared Writing time, you may want to discuss the many different kinds of shoes and make a word web together. You could also do this with a small group at the shoe store.

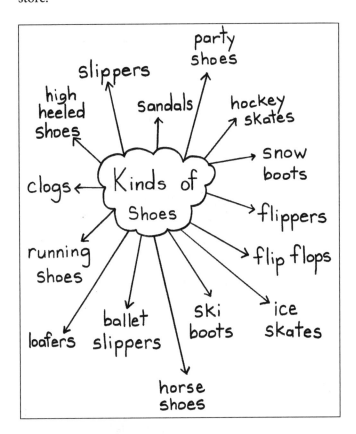

This is the sort of word web that the teacher and children might create at a Shared Writing time.

Invite the children to search their homes and bring in examples of all these shoes, as well as empty shoeboxes to add to the centre. Cut out 8 to 10 footprints of various sizes and label them with corresponding numbers. Order them from smallest to largest and have them available at the centre so that the salesperson can measure the customer's foot for the appropriate size. You might even want to tape these feet to the floor so customers can measure their own feet.

In addition to the various shoes and boxes, add short and long shoehorns, rags to polish the shoes, and shoetrees. Since many children are likely unfamiliar with these terms, be sure to present and discuss these items in the large group before adding them to the centre. Through role-play, the children will quickly learn to use them in context.

A shoe-store setting opens up possibilities for a number of other literacy-related activities:

- Read *Whose Shoe?* by Margaret Miller in the large group and then at the Drawing/Writing centre let interested children make individual books modelled on the simple patterned text.
- Try taking photographs of the many shoes in your collection, and use them to make a matching game involving image and corresponding word.
- Have a vote to determine the name of the shoe store and then prompt the children to make a large mural of the name — for example, Shoes R Us — to hang in the centre.
- Be sure to extend the language development by including a cash register, sales tags, and prices for the shoes. Including a phone for the store is also helpful because sales associates may need to call another store to check on a particular size!

Other retail stores: Other stores that have provided effective settings for dramatic play include grocery and flower stores. A grocery store can be made authentic by including small carts, local store flyers, and recycled, cardboard cereal, cracker, and pasta boxes, as well as plastic pop bottles, ice-cream containers, and yogurt cups. A flower shop can become very dynamic by having plastic flowers and plastic vases, as well as labels and prices — Roses $5, Mums $3. A neighborhood florist might be willing to donate various sizes of flower boxes for delivery. Collect bulb catalogues and books about flowers. Use stickers to create a Concentration or a matching game to encourage visual discrimination and visual memory. (See Appendix B: Games for instructions on how to make and use the game.)

Hairdresser/Barber shop

During a Shared Writing experience, create a large menu including the various services that might be offered at a hairdresser or barber shop. You can expect the children to give you such words as *trim, cut, bangs, color, highlights, beard, braid, French braid* and *updo,* and you can note a few simple services they do not identify. You might list these services on a style chart along with their prices. This price list could also be presented in a smaller format as a receipt after the service has been provided. Having a cash register to receive payment and provide change is a good idea. There could also be an appointment book, as well as a telephone, to record and read appointment times.

To ensure proper hygiene, the children should not be brushing and combing their own or each other's hair; instead, they can brush and comb dolls' hair. These dolls can each be placed in a high chair and arranged in front of a plastic mirror. Several high chairs and mirrors could be lined up along a wall to create the look of a salon. In addition, the children could style wigs or plastic busts that are created to encourage children to style hair. This centre should include various sizes of brushes and combs, as well as plastic scissors, headbands, hair clips, hair elastics, and ribbons. All of these items should be kept in labelled bins to encourage sight vocabulary. Empty shampoo, conditioner, hairspray, and gel bottles can add to the drama and authenticity. Provide the children with smocks to cover the dolls' bodies and catch the "hairs." Of course, a broom and dustpan are necessary to sweep up all the "hair clippings."

Obtaining Centre Resources

Asking the children to bring in items from home is an effective way of equipping a centre; however, this approach also is valuable because it involves the children and their families in the operation of the centre. Dollar stores can be invaluable sources of items too. Teachers typically collect items over time and often share with other colleagues.

The Hair Salon

Name RaCHEL

Price 12 $DOLRS

Appointment Time 5ThRTe

Style S PoneeS

Simple forms such as this one engage children in play-related writing. Here, a child has recorded that she expects to pay $12 at a 5:30 appointment for two "ponies" — ponytails.

Doctor's office

Line up several chairs against the wall in the centre to help create a waiting room fully equipped with magazines, picture books, and toys for young patients. Provide a desk and chair for a nurse/receptionist to check health-card information. (The same setup could be used for a dentist's office.) To create the image of the doctor's actual office, turn all the Home/Dramatic Play centre furniture around to face the wall and cover it with white sheets. Add tensor bandages, band aids, old casts, X-rays, plastic stethoscopes, otoscopes, and thermometers. Be sure to make a place for each of these items and label it with the appropriate word so that the children can have this matching experience when they are dramatizing, as well as tidying up. You might also have a small group of children create a large eye-exam chart that can be posted on the wall along with the doctor's name and medical degrees.

Provide the children with fictitious medical pads, as well as medical charts on clipboards, so that they can role-play the doctor and the patient. Let them make use of a date stamp. Below is a filled-in sample template for a prescription form.

The Doctor's Office

Patient's Name _Pete_

Medicine _Pfr_

Instructions _takn ye._

Doctor's Name _DB_

The child playing doctor has directed the patient to take a puffer when he feels wheezy.

Veterinarian's office

Children love to care for animals and transforming the Home/Dramatic Play centre into a veterinarian's office can be very effective. The impetus for this extension may be the news that one of the children in the class has a new pet. With this news other children typically begin to talk about their pets. You may want to read *Franklin Gets a Pet* by Paulette Bourgeois and *I Love Animals* by Flora McDonnell and then hold a vote to determine which book the children like best. This vote could be recorded on a simple T-chart with a photocopy of the cover of each book at the top of the chart. Have the children write their names under the book cover they like the best. Discuss the results.

During a large-group time, prompt the children to engage in a Think-Pair-Share experience to discuss the pets in their lives. "Talk about an animal you have or wish you could have." Through this discussion, the children will generate a list of various kinds of animals, including a bird, rabbit, cat, dog, hamster, gerbil, guinea pig, horse, cow, and pig. The names of these animals can be recorded.

Gather stuffed animals of various sizes to become the patients in the veterinarian's office. Place a large white sheet over the furniture in the centre to create the effect of a vet's office and add bandages, casts, X-rays, collars, and a plastic doctor's kit. Strips of white cloth or Velcro can work well as reusable casts. Provide several large white shirts to serve as lab coats for staff.

Much as a doctor's office might have, the veterinarian's office would benefit from having an appointment book and a medical pad, as well as a cash register and a telephone. The office could also include a sign to show hours of operation and prices for various services, including the giving of shots and vitamins, setting of broken bones, treating of cuts, and operations.

Bank

Go for a class walk around the community and record all the different kinds of banks. To help prepare for this centre, enter several banks and ask to have some letterhead, brochures, and posters to add to it. One way to introduce the centre is by reading *Bunny Money* by Rosemary Wells and then working with the children to list all the different kinds of North American coins. Try referencing non-fiction books about other countries and discuss the different kinds of money around the world — for example, pounds sterling in England, dollars in the United States, and yen in Japan. Invite the children to bring some of these monies to school; after a child has presented a type of money to the class, you might tape it to a poster for the children to examine and compare.

Transform the Home centre into a bank by arranging the furniture to create a teller counter where the banker works on one side and the customer to be served stands on the other. Add several money trays filled with play money and challenge the children to sort the paper money and coins into the various denominations. Provide the children with void deposit and withdrawal slips and void cheques, as well as notepads to record a name and transaction amount. You may want to devise your own cheque template.

Campsite

Reading *Curious George Goes Camping* by Margret and H. A. Rey to the large group can provide the impetus for introducing a campsite setting. Try pitching a tent in the centre and invite the children to role-play a family on a summer camping trip. Add several coolers and some plastic food, as well as a picnic blanket, sleeping bags, blankets, flashlights, books, and maps to read.

It can be effective to hang a clothesline and attach towels and other items with clothes pegs. These items can be arranged by color, size, or word feature: for example, hang the shirts, shorts, and socks together because the words all start with the letter *s*.

The presence of a campsite centre for dramatic play also ties in with a number of large-group and other centre activities.

- Read the chant in Michael Rosen's *We're Going on a Bear Hunt* (illustrated by Helen Oxenbury) and then invite the children to create their own version titled "We're Going on a Camping Trip." Have the children add mime to each section of the chant.
- In a large group, play the circle memory game "I Went Camping and I Saw . . . ." Each child in turn repeats the previous child's idea and then adds another, creating a cumulative story.
- Challenge the children to work co-operatively in a small group at the Visual Arts centre to paint a mural to display at the campsite centre. This mural might include a night-time camping scene complete with tall trees, black sky, stars, fireworks, campfire, squirrels, and owls. Have the children use a sponge-painting technique to create a background (see Appendix C: Recipes for Visual Arts Activities). Let them finish the mural by adding words to label the items painted or captions to explain their function, for example, a tent to sleep in, a picnic table to eat at, a campfire to roast marshmallows on.
- With the large group, make a list of camping foods, including sandwiches, fruit, hot dogs, and the ever popular S'mores. During a large-group Shared Writing experience, take the opportunity to print the ingredients for S'mores (at left).

Print, as well, "How to Make S'mores" to help the children role-play the making of the recipe. Providing the steps can be a meaningful way to introduce procedural writing. Help the children to read the words as necessary. Be sure to add illustrations to aid in the reading and post the recipe at the campsite centre.

School

Read the favorite *Chrysanthemum* by Kevin Henkes or *Spot Goes to School* by Eric Hill and then discuss all the furniture and special items associated with a school. Arrange the furniture in the temporary centre to reflect the children's suggestions, perhaps providing an easel and small carpet for large-group teaching, a grouping of desks where the children can write, and a bulletin board to display and celebrate the children's efforts. Big Books and pointers, as well as an attendance folder with a class list, can help the children identify familiar words.

Creating an Environment for Success in the Home/Dramatic Play Centre

The following section is presented in terms of questions that the reflective practitioner is encouraged to ask about the classroom's Home/Dramatic Play centre. The answers reflect what we have found to be best practices.

1. How do I ensure that the Home/Dramatic Play centre remains inviting and organized?

- Allocate enough space for the children to have adequate room to play.

S'mores

Ingredients
graham crackers
marshmallows
chocolate chips

How to Make S'mores

1. Build a pretend fire using logs and red and orange tissue paper.
2. Place a marshmallow on the end of a stick.
3. Roast the marshmallow over the fake fire.
4. Place the marshmallow on a graham cracker.
5. Add chocolate chips.
6. Add another graham cracker on top.
7. Enjoy!

- Add materials of good quality and discard broken or worn items.
- Organize the Home centre so that all materials have a specific, marked place.
- Select materials that represent the cultures and family structures of the children in the class (e.g., children and single parent, children and grandparents).
- Introduce other materials that represent the broader community (e.g., paella pans).
- Encourage the children to bring items from home to add to the centre.
- Involve the children in determining the number of people who can safely and productively use the centre in each of its changing settings. After an initial trial, discuss how well the agreed-upon number worked.
- Continually review and modify the routines.

2. How do I ensure that the tidy up is successful and that it remains the responsibility of the children?

- Consider the centre's location and the traffic flow within the room. You will want to ensure that the centre is not disruptive and does not interfere with other centres in the room. A corner is often effective.
- Carefully lay out the materials in an organized and labelled manner before the children are introduced to the centre.
- Discuss new materials and establish new routines and expectations related to the latest transformation of the centre.
- Give children extra time so they can be responsible for the tidy up.
- Ask other children to be monitors to check the centre after the tidy up.

3. How do I evaluate the children's role-playing?

- Refer to the suggested mileposts below to guide your observations. Remember that each child will not necessarily demonstrate all of the suggested mileposts.
- Record how often the children voluntarily choose the centre.
- Take note of the circumstances under which the children demonstrate the observed behaviors. Is it regularly with teacher direction and support, or rarely?
- Take note of how well the children demonstrate the observed skills, knowledge, or behavior. Do they do so reluctantly or confidently?

4. How do I help to ensure that parents value the centre as much as work in the Drawing/Writing centre or Reading centre?

- Share your knowledge and enthusiasm about the importance of providing opportunities for the children to express themselves through drama.
- Demonstrate how much you value the centre by spending as much time adding to it, changing it, and talking about it as you do for a Drawing/Writing centre or Reading centre.
- Schedule time for you to visit the centre.
- Regularly share your observations of the learning with the children and their parents. You might discuss literacy skills, for example, saying, "Jamie confidently prints his name on tallies and voting charts."
- On every occasion, including parents' night and in newsletters, take the opportunity to draw the parents' attention to the possible learning. For example, show parents the various templates for the Home/Dramatic Play centre extensions.

- Provide evidence of the children's learning in their portfolios and on bulletin boards. Use photographs, videos, audiotapes, and samples of their reading, writing, and drawings.
- Encourage the parents to contribute materials for the centre.
- Invite parents to volunteer. For example, parents are often willing to help the children do baking and cooking, such as making real pizzas in the restaurant.
- Track the children's progress and share their development with the parents on a regular basis. You can use Post-it notes and a page for each child to record observations and learning.

Mileposts to Help Guide Teacher Observations of Children Engaged in Role-Play

The developmental mileposts outlined here are guidelines only — they are not intended to be all-inclusive or prescriptive. They can be very useful in helping teachers assess children's developmental levels, plan appropriate demonstrations, and offer timely feedback. We used them for observation and assessment and to plan effective teaching strategies in the Kindergarten classroom.

How children show an interest in role-play

Children interested in role-play choose to role-play. They willingly join in the role-play when invited by the teacher or other classmates and continue to role-play over time. Interested children will bring items from home to support their role-play. They will also ask the teacher, other classmates, their parents, and visitors to take part in the role-play.

How children approach role-play

Over time, children will become more involved in role-play and in their relations with other children. Typical milestones are as follows:

- watching other children role-play but remaining uninvolved
- role-playing alone and ignoring or remaining oblivious to the other children
- role-playing near other children, using the same materials but not becoming involved with others
- role-playing beside other children, sharing the equipment, experiences, or ideas, but continuing to be concerned with their own play and having little interest in what others are doing
- role-playing co-operatively with other children, sometimes assuming both leadership and follower roles
- role-playing co-operatively with other children, often planning and carrying out joint plans

Literacy skills that children demonstrate when they role-play

- Children use language to express their feelings and to sort out problems in new situations. For example, a child says, "The baby is crying. Maybe she needs food or a diaper change."
- Children use language in appropriate contexts, such as "I need to blow up an air mattress."
- Children use language for a variety of purposes, for example, to retell, reflect, relate, direct, describe, question, or inform.

- Children use language in a variety of familiar and imaginary situations. For example, a child says, "I will be the veterinarian, and you can bring in your sick dog for an appointment and a shot of medicine."
- Children draw, read, and write to support their role-playing. For example, they might take a phone message on a note pad.
- Children may use books, charts, lists, labels, templates, and so on for reference.

Behaviors that children demonstrate when they role-play

Child behaviors to look for include the following:

- assuming familiar roles (e.g., mommy, daddy)
- assuming imaginary roles (e.g., teacher, camper, doctor, princess)
- using familiar materials to support the role-play (e.g., dolls)
- using new materials to support the role-play (e.g., a stethoscope for a doctor, a flashlight for a camper)
- sharing materials
- creating props from materials in the room (e.g., a paper chef's hat)
- taking on a variety of roles (The teacher can encourage this by saying something like this: "Both boys and girls can have turns being pilots, hairdressers, shoe sales staff, and parents.")
- solving problems (Example: "We can't both be the chef, so you be the customer this time and then we'll switch.")
- including others in the play
- taking turns

The Home/Dramatic Play centre is unique in its ability to engage children with language, both oral and written. Through their dramatizations, the children re-enact and explore real-life experiences with everyday relationships and familiar tasks and roles. Teachers can capitalize on this involvement and use these opportunities to help the children develop their communication skills of listening, speaking, viewing, reading, and writing.

7

The Sand Centre

Sand is appealing to all children. Even very young children gain satisfaction and success when touching and playing with sand. It soothes and pleases their senses. It is intriguing and extends their curiosity and creativity.

In the Sand centre, there are more excellent literacy opportunities than would be available from simply completing literacy worksheets. The sand helps the children to develop a myriad of literacy knowledge, skills, and attitudes. Activities at this centre provide considerable, meaningful, and connected opportunities for children to acquire new vocabulary. By listening, reading, writing, co-operating, experimenting, dramatizing, and observing, the children re-enact familiar, real-life experiences and roles.

Here, a child has recorded time spent at the Sand centre.

The Sand centre is a place where children can explore mathematical, scientific, and technological concepts, as well as literacy learning. Work in the sand allows children to explore these concepts hands-on, providing the foundation for later abstract thinking. The very nature of sand fascinates children — it invites exploration, experimentation, and problem solving. Children can develop eye-hand coordination and small muscle control. In addition, they learn and use the language of mathematics, science, and technology. In a Kindergarten classroom, there are, of course, children with many different kinds of background experiences and developmental levels.

Some children have had many experiences with sand; others have had only limited ones. As a result, children are always seeing new behaviors to imitate. Experimentation and investigation flourish in such an atmosphere where the children are expected, but not pressured, to explore. At this centre, many informal discussions take place, and the more experienced users willingly and naturally answer the questions of less sophisticated sand users, who might ask, "Where does this belong?" or "How do I get more water to make a lake?"

Depending on the current interest, the teacher makes many books, both fiction and non-fiction, available at the Sand centre, and these resources inform the children's work. For example, perhaps the children decide to create a "beach" environment in the sand. During a Shared Writing experience, the children might brainstorm what creatures can be seen at the beach — for example, ducks, geese, herons, crabs, crayfish, jellyfish, sandpipers, and seagulls. After adding models of these creatures to the sand table, the children might also refer to a related non-fiction book and add the book to a table near this beach environment. They can then use this information to gather and name or label various models of creatures that they and the teacher have added to the beach environment. *On the Beach*, an Usborne Lift-the-Flap Book by Alistair Smith, is a valuable resource to share.

Introducing the Sand Centre

Sand Centre Routines

Respect the limitations on the number of children permitted at the centre.
Sweep up the sand after use.
Brush the sand off the tools.
Return each tool to the correct labelled space on a table or shelf.
Put the plastic letters that spell S A N D in the sand to signify that the centre has been tidied up.

We found that the second week of Kindergarten was a good time to introduce the Sand centre, which we typically did before the Water centre. An engaging way to introduce the centre is by reading aloud *Bears at the Beach* by Niki Yektai or a suitable, related book suggested by your teacher-librarian. We recommend beginning the year with no tools in the centre because doing so helps to establish the routines and allows the children to use their hands to explore the properties of wet and dry sand. In our classrooms, children freely explored their own interests, creating tunnels, mounds, or landscapes.

As we observed the children in their use of the sand, we added materials and tools that would enable them to further develop concepts and skills. For example, to help children understand volume, we added bowls of different sizes and shapes. We slowly introduced these materials at the large-group time, so the children would be familiar with the items and the expected routines.

Materials That Encourage Literacy Learning at the Sand Centre

The following kinds of materials are helpful:

- commercial and "found" materials of varying sizes to accommodate the different degrees of grip and control of children of different stages of development and experience: kitchen utensils, garden tools, different-sized plastic containers, and cardboard paper-towel tubes (ideal for pouring, tunnelling, making silos, and pouring cement)
- props, such as miniature animals, people, and dinosaurs
- materials from the natural environment, such as rocks, twigs, and shells
- materials to extend children's explorations, for example, magnifying glasses, scales, measurement containers, sieves, funnels, string, rope and pulleys

- materials for recording, including pencils, graph paper with squares, Post-its, clipboards, pieces of acrylic with overhead markers for writing, mini-chalk-boards, and white boards
- materials for cleanup, such as a dustpan, small and large brooms and brushes
- related books and reference materials, both fiction and non-fiction

---

Books for the Sand Centre

Non-fiction We Found Useful

- *The Amazing Dirt Book* by Paulette Bourgeois and Valerie Wyatt
- *The Quicksand Book* by Tomie dePaola
- *Digging Up Dinosaurs* by Aliki
- *Talk About Sand* by Angela Webb

Fiction We Found Helpful

- *Puddleman* by Ted Staunton
- *Mud* by Mary Lyn Ray
- *Sea, Sand, Me* by Patricia Hubbell
- *My New Sandbox* by Donna Jakob
- *Bears at the Beach* by Niki Yektai

The Sand centre can be rich in resources, both tools and props. In our Kindergarten classrooms, we had tools for digging, burying, filling, pouring, sifting, measuring, moulding, scraping, and constructing, and these were stored in labelled bins. To encourage oral language and dramatic play, we made available many props, such as cars, trucks, planes, multiracial models of people, animals, twigs, string, and clipboards for recording. We did not, however, have all of these materials available at the same time.

We recommend structuring the learning around an interest that emerges from the children and extends to the Sand centre. If, for example, the children express a particular interest in vehicles, you might select a favorite book about vehicles, such as *Trucks* by Byron Barton, and use it as an incentive to transform the Sand centre into a local community, a highway, or a garage.

Literacy Activities in the Sand Centre

Game ideas include Concentration, where, for example, the children match pictures and words from a beach environment; and Jaws, perhaps between a meat-eating and a plant-eating dinosaur. Appendix B: Games outlines these flexible structures.

All the learning at the Sand centre can be enriched, supported, and extended through various literacy activities. The centre provides many opportunities for literacy experiences that involve listening, speaking, reading, writing, and media awareness. It can become an excellent springboard for the development of oral language, as well as reading, writing, and viewing skills. Especially with the infusion of related texts, charts, games, models, videos, and authentic artifacts (e.g., sticks, shells, leaves, and stones), the Sand centre can effectively promote literacy learning.

The suggestions outlined below are based on successful experiences in various dynamic Kindergarten classrooms and can stimulate a renewed interest in the Sand centre. Note that a classroom Sand centre would not be transformed into *all* these variations during one school year. Instead, the teacher would select the activities that best suited the needs of the children. Depending on the interest shown by the children, a literacy extension might last for a few days or longer. The extensions used in any classroom are dependent on time, availability of materials, and the interests of the children and teacher.

Bakery in the sand

To introduce this extension, you might read *Spot Bakes a Cake* by Eric Hill at the read-aloud time and then, during a Shared Writing session, make a list of all the things that the children might want to bake, perhaps cookies, brownies, muffins, cupcakes, and loaves.

At the centre, be sure to have baking sheets, rolling pins, mixing bowls, wooden spoons, spatulas, paper muffin cups, and measuring spoons and cups to help the children explore the baking process. Authentic flour packages, as well as cookie and brownie containers, make the children feel like real bakers. Providing a disposable crepe-paper chef's hat and an apron can stimulate imagination, dramatization, and oral language development. You might create recipes with the children and post them close to the Sand centre as a reading resource.

The learning at the Sand centre can be highlighted through literacy games. For example, all the items at the bakery can be used to create a Concentration game. Teachers often use commercial Concentration games and while these are effective, producing them with the specific vocabulary that the children are generating makes the learning even more meaningful. Involving capable children in the creation of such games can result in exciting learning for them.

Vehicles in the sand

You might begin by reading *The Day Duck's Truck Got Stuck* by Maria Fleming (illustrated by Rusty Fletcher). In a large or small group, create a word web of all the different types of vehicles that the children know (see the example in Appendix A: Ways to Record Ideas). Have the children illustrate the web and post the chart as a reference at the Sand centre. Stimulate discussion by adding props such as miniature cars, vans, trucks, motorcycle, bicycles, and buses to the Sand centre — Duplo makes an excellent, sturdy collection of vehicles and service workers in the community. Try adding pieces of string to the sand so the children can use them to outline the spaces in a parking lot or garage.

Zoo in the sand

During a class trip to the zoo, challenge the children to obtain a pictorial site map of the zoo and use it to find their favorite animals — encourage them to hold on to it. Upon return to the classroom, read aloud *Dear Zoo* by Rod Campbell, a delightful, lift-the-flap book with simple, predictable, and repetitive text, to the large group. Such a book will help young learners to have success with books and see themselves as real readers.

Let children create a zoo in the sand, using the map from the zoo or one found on the Internet. Add models of zoo animals, plastic berry containers for cages, and sticks to the centre. Provide labelled containers that the children can use for sorting and placing all the same animals (e.g., giraffes). They thereby gain experience matching objects with words. These labelled containers will also facilitate the tidy up. The animal words can be used to make a Tic-Tac-Toe game (see Appendix B: Games for more information).

Farm in the sand

One way to introduce the farm extension is through the song "Old McDonald Had a Farm," which most of the children will have heard. Print the song on chart paper or on a whiteboard, and read and sing the song together. Add models of farm animals, books about the farm, and a model barn to the Sand centre.

Another way to have the children think about farm animals is to read a picture book by Nancy Tafuri. *Silly Little Goose!* tells the tale of a goose looking for a home on a farm. The goose explores the chicken coop, the pigpen, and other animals' homes until finally she finds a place to lay her eggs. Ask the children to predict where they think she will find a place to nest. The children quickly "read" the sounds that individual animals make to shoo the goose away. In addition, during a Shared Writing experience, you might create a T-chart to sort and classify wild and farm animals.

You could also provide a blank Venn diagram for the purpose of classifying all animals (e.g., pet, wild, and farm). This Venn diagram provides an opportunity for differentiated instruction. Using hula hoops with models or pictures of animals works well. (See Appendix A: Ways to Record Ideas.)

This Venn diagram shows animals that live in the water (dolphin, fish), animals that live on the land (zebra, cat, dog) and animals that can live in both places (frog, snake).

Exploring the story: "The 3 Little Pigs"

At several Gathering Times, read aloud various versions of the classic story "The 3 Little Pigs" and then add appropriate materials to the sand to promote retelling of the story. You might provide models of three plastic pigs and a wolf, as well as pieces of straw, Popsicle sticks, and small Lego pieces to build the three houses.

With a small group of children, create a map of the story to model retelling and help the children develop story sequence and an understanding of beginning, middle, and end of a story. Use a horizontal strip of paper. Usually, the title is recorded in the far left panel and about five aspects of the story are illustrated in the remaining frames — the story map should fold like an accordion. More advanced literacy learners might use pictures and words to make their own story maps.

You can also add a fun game to this extension, where the wolf tries to catch the pig! (See Appendix B: Games for details on how to make and play Jaws.)

Here is a child's legend for a grid of animals buried in the sand.

Sand centre work has prompted a child to print the words for *turtle, frog,* and *snake* — they appear backwards. The rectangle, triangle, and circle, far right, indicate what the reader should look for on the child's marker-printed grid.

The Sand centre provides many opportunities to explore aspects of science. Children can think about dinosaurs, farm animals, and wild animals. They can also explore various concepts such as those related to measuring and digging.

Dinosaurs in the sand

Read aloud fiction and non-fiction books about dinosaurs and then transform the Sand centre into a palaeontologist's research site. Begin the adventure by saying something like this to the large group: "Some scientists like to do research on dinosaurs. They are called 'palaeontologists' because the word *paleo* means ancient or prehistoric. What do you think a palaeontologist does?" Record the children's ideas in chart form and add related items to the Sand centre — goggles, small and large brushes, white coats, bugs, and plastic dinosaurs. Bury models of dinosaurs in the sand. Use string to create a grid in the sand and provide the children with a grid template to record where each dinosaur was uncovered. Devise a Bingo game using the new terminology from this extension of the Sand centre. (For more information on how to do this and play this game, see Appendix B: Games.)

Creating an animal habitat

One way to introduce this extension is to read *Tunnels* by Gail Gibbons; then, add paper-towel rolls and toilet-paper rolls to the sand, which should be 15 cm to 20 cm deep (6 to 8 inches). The presence of these materials will invite the children to dig, tunnel, and explore. During large-group times, you can extend an interest in tunnels by reading books about animals that burrow and tunnel to make their homes — these include rabbits, rats, moles, and groundhogs. *Let's All Dig and Burrow* by Anna Nilsen and *My Very First Book of Animal Homes* by Eric Carle are appropriate titles to share, but teachers and children can check their library/ resource centres for other related titles. When the interest of the children wanes, you might want to store the materials in a bin for children to use at a later time.

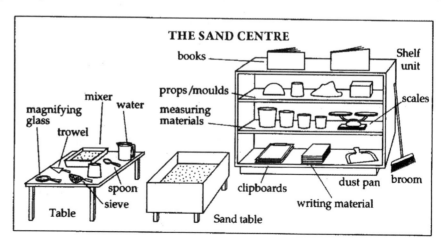

THE SAND CENTRE

Creating an Environment for Success in the Sand Centre

The following section is presented in terms of questions that the reflective practitioner is encouraged to ask about the classroom's Sand centre. The answers reflect what we have found to be best practices.

1. How do I ensure that the Sand centre remains inviting and challenging to children in different stages of development?

- Introduce materials for different purposes: digging, pouring, moulding, moving, sifting, measuring, recording, and dramatic play.
- Regularly add more materials that extend the concepts with which the children are experimenting. Try adding rulers, pieces of Planko, Kapla, wooden blocks, and Popsicle sticks. These materials will invite the children to make connections and explore different kinds of bridges.
- Remember always to introduce any new routine or materials to the whole group, reinforcing the concepts many times.
- Reorganize the storage of the materials used to date, so that the shapes of new materials can be outlined on a table or shelf.
- Group materials into labelled baskets or boxes according to their purpose, ranging from moulding or pouring to serving as props for dramatic play.
- You might remove the used materials and put out new materials that are linked to another specific interest.

2. What is my role as teacher in relation to the Sand centre?

- Introduce any new materials or routines to the whole group over time.
- Plan for Cambourne's conditions of learning to occur — responsibility, immersion, expectation, demonstration, meaningful practice, approximation, and feedback or positive response.
- Plan for specific learning to occur. For example, after hearing the children talking about dinosaurs and bringing in models from home, read about dinosaurs and then at a Shared Writing time, make a T-chart that classifies the dinosaurs as meat eaters or plant eaters. Encourage the children to make a dinosaur habitat, complete with hills, trees, and water, grouping the dinosaurs according to their classification. Another way to classify dinosaurs is to decide whether they are land, water, or flying creatures. Any chart that the class makes might be added to the centre for the children to use when they are creating different sites. Use both pictures and vocabulary that you and the children have generated. (See Appendix A: Ways to Record Ideas for information about various ways to record information.)
- Take the time to observe individuals and small groups of children as they work.
- Record your observations, keeping in mind the learning expectations of the curriculum in your jurisdiction. Use a notebook with a page for each student for your observations. Be sure to take photographs to document the children's work.
- Be available to extend the learning. Sit with, listen to, pose, and answer questions, and generally interact with the children, modelling and introducing new concepts and skills.
- Direct the children to their peers for information and help.
- Ensure that the materials are appropriate and well maintained.

3. How do I ensure that the Sand centre is safe?

- Make sure the sand that the children are using meets safety standards. Avoid sand that is high in silica content and order through your Board.
- Consider the location of this centre — keep it away from the Water centre. Limit the use of water available to add to the sand. Provide a container of water before the activity period begins and tell the children who need more water than provided to speak with you.
- Introduce the children to the routines and expectations for the centre. Do this often! For example, you will want to encourage regular sweeping to reduce slippage since sand often spills onto the floor with normal use.
- Redirect the children who continually misuse the sand (e.g., throwing the sand or not tidying up). Initially, reinforce the routines of the Sand centre in the large group and remind children individually of their responsibilities. If misuse continues, redirect the children to another activity.
- Regularly check the materials for breakage, damage, and cleanliness.
- Discuss with the children how many of them can safely use this centre. The number will vary depending on the size of the sandbox and space available. Post a sign including pictures and numbers to remind the children how many may work at the centre.
- Ensure that the Sand centre is within your hearing and sight as this centre can sometimes require a great deal of adult supervision.

Mileposts to Help Guide Teacher Observations of Children Working with the Sand

These developmental mileposts are guidelines only — they are not intended to be all-inclusive or prescriptive; they can, however, be tremendously informative in guiding teacher interaction with children and in planning for extensions.

Ways that children show their interest in the sand

Children demonstrate their interest by the choices they make and the responsibilities they take. They might choose the Sand centre as an activity, willingly experiment and explore the properties of sand, and also take risks, perhaps saying, "Let's see what will happen when we add more water." Interested children will follow the routines and accept responsibility for their own behavior. They also concentrate for a reasonable time. Using a variety of tools, they might work alone or co-operatively share, take turns, and exchange ideas. They might help other children solve problems and tidy up.

Literacy skills that children demonstrate in the Sand centre

There are many literacy skills that children might demonstrate.

- Children examine the scientific books or photographs provided.
- Children talk about the ideas in the books and what they are doing in the sand. You can encourage this by using some of the vocabulary appropriate to the play, for example, saying, "I see that you are creating a habitat for your dinosaurs." In response, a child might say, "Yes, I'm putting the brontosaurus over here in the trees because he is a plant eater, and I have some leaves over here for him to eat."

- Children retell, relate, and make connections. Encourage this by using some of the vocabulary appropriate to the play. As an example: "When we went to the beach, we saw a lot of sandpipers. They were running so fast we couldn't catch them."
- Children refer to books, photographs, or videos for information and ideas to inform their play.
- Children help to make a list of sand words — for example, *sift, mould, pour, pat*. You can post these words on a chart at the Sand centre or compile them into a class book with photographs.
- Children choose to read class-developed materials about sand during their private reading time.
- They use their imaginations to create a landscape.
- They use signs provided by the teacher and developed with the large group to extend the play, for example, a sign for a garage, a barn, or a tunnel.
- They make signs to label their work.
- They record discoveries and results of simple experiments and work. For example, you could provide the children with grid paper to record the placement of each of the buried animals in the dinosaur world; model the process using large chart or grid paper at a Shared Writing session.
- Children write narrative or expository text to describe their work. A beginning piece of writing might be a bristol board sign saying
    IMDACV
    for "I made a cave."
- Children play the language games that have been introduced and demonstrated by the teacher to the whole group.
- They apply new knowledge to other situations. For example, they might add signs from the Drawing/Writing centre or locate a related book on topic from the school's library/resource centre.

Other skills that children demonstrate

Children might do any of the following:
- feeling the sand; letting it run through their fingers
- moving, patting, moulding, and digging sand; burying objects in it
- using tools with control to scrape, pat, move, and dig
- using other materials to move the sand (e.g., funnels, spoons, scoops, pulleys)
- recognizing and talking about the properties of sand (For example, dry sand can be poured and wet sand can be moulded.)
- pouring from one container to another, eventually with control
- filling containers of various sizes, eventually with control
- comparing amounts of sand (e.g., more, less, same)
- using non-standard materials to compare quantity (e.g., containers of different sizes)
- using standardized materials to measure (e.g., graduated containers, simple scales, measuring spoons)

Other knowledge that children demonstrate

Knowledge that children might demonstrate includes the following:

- recognizing the different properties of the sand (e.g., wet and dry, coarse or fine)

- recognizing the possibilities for the uses of the different tools (For example, a sifter allows one to separate the sand from other items; a funnel helps one pour more accurately.)
- using appropriate language to describe, compare, draw conclusions, predict, estimate, and direct
- exploring new mathematical and scientific concepts and vocabulary (e.g., *volume, mass, cause and effect*)

Children are naturally drawn to sand. The Sand centre in a Kindergarten classroom provides endless opportunities for children to develop literacy skills as well as other skills. In the sand, children explore and experiment and then use oral language to describe their efforts. These understandings can be recorded using pictures and words and then extended through fiction and non-fiction text. Sand is a wonderful vehicle to stimulate language development.

8 The Water Centre

Water, like sand, is a medium that all children instinctively find appealing. It intrigues them, appeals to their senses, and is soothing to their touch. Playing with water is a familiar activity since from an early age, children have taken delight in splashing in puddles, running through the garden sprinkler, and blowing bubbles. Once children are acclimatized to the feel of water, bath time often becomes a time of great enjoyment and learning. They naturally splash and move their toys through the water, manipulating and exploring its properties. Through the unstructured play in the home, children begin to experiment with and learn about the properties of water. This familiarity helps make the transfer from home to school easier.

In the Kindergarten classroom, the Water centre builds on children's natural interest in water. The centre becomes a place where children at all stages of development can experience success. In addition to developing eye-hand coordination and small muscle control, the very nature of water activities invites the children to explore, experiment, and problem-solve. Playing with water also affords children the chance to explore and begin to understand mathematical, scientific, and technological concepts such as flotation, measurement, and displacement in a hands-on way.

Through their experiences with water in the Kindergarten, children have many opportunities for language and literacy development. They use new vocabulary as they make predictions, test their hypotheses, share their findings, and learn to record their observations in a logical, scientific manner. By talking, listening, writing, reading, co-operating, dramatizing, experimenting, and observing, they develop critical skills, knowledge, and values in the areas of literacy, mathematics, science, and technology.

Introducing the Water Centre

We recommend introducing the Water centre by reading a variety of fiction and non-fiction books during group time. For example, we sometimes began with reading *Puddles* by Jonathan London during a Shared Reading time; then, we introduced a Shared Writing experience by brainstorming a list of all the places where the children might have experienced or seen water, for example, a swimming pool, bathtub, pond, river, or beach. This list was later posted at the Water centre for children to refer to and read.

We found it worked best to open up this centre with only water, cleanup materials, and cups of various sizes to explore the movement and properties of the water. Presenting a limited number of materials provides the children with time and opportunity to explore and experiment, unhampered by the constraints of specific tools.

We introduced new tools — for example, water wheels, pumps, and funnels — and talked about expectations for use and tidy up during group times — demonstrating how tidy up will occur is important. We continued to reinforce the routines on an individual basis during activity time. As soon as routines were fully established, we began to introduce a small quantity of tools on shelves or a table in the Water centre. To facilitate tidy up, we traced around each tool and labelled each place.

Those children who had prior experience with water were invaluable in motivating other children to experiment. Through their language, together with the teacher's, they provided many informal demonstrations; they also answered questions, offered a helping hand, set new challenges, shared the problem solving, and extended the learning. Less experienced water users gained a great deal by imitating the behaviors and language of the more sophisticated users. The more experienced learners benefited, too. When they explained, described, and shared their knowledge, they consolidated their own understandings. For example, one child might say to another, "The more soap you add to the water, the more bubbles you will get." Together, children of all levels of competence made predictions, solved problems, and shared their findings.

We encouraged the children to use this medium to set their own challenges, express these challenges aloud, and then with our help select those tools that would help them to solve these problems. For example, a child might say, "I want to find out if all the plastic things like mine sink." As the children gained experience, we carefully added selected materials, such as those items that might float or sink. Focusing on specific scientific concepts helped the children to extend their oral and reading vocabulary as they made predictions and observed the results. Some children were also able to record their findings in picture form or in writing. They might use a T-chart to record the objects that floated on one side and the objects that sank on the other side. (See Appendix A: Ways to Record Ideas.)

Things That Float	Things That Sink
JEGO	SN
SPN	PNE
STC	

On his T-chart, a child named Sebastian recorded that Lego, spoons, and a stick float, but that a stone and a penny sink.

Water words

Here are some water topics to consider when interacting with the children on an individual basis or during large-group discussion time. The children can generate vocabulary associated with these ideas:

- water (e.g., *rain, ice, hail, sleet, snow, mist, steam, boil, freeze, melt, pour, overflow, spill, sprinkle, splash*)
- uses of water (e.g., *drinking, bathing, cleaning, irrigating, swimming, boating, skiing, fighting fires, growing plants and flowers*)

This waterdrop-shaped page in a class book notes that water can be found in a hot tub.

- kinds of water (e.g., *clean, muddy, still, carbonated, hot, cold, frozen*)
- bodies of water (e.g., *puddle, lake, stream, river, ocean, sea, brook, rapids, canal*)
- water pollution (e.g., *oil spill, chemicals, sewage, garbage*)

Materials That Encourage Literacy Learning at the Water Centre

Essential to the Water centre is a large water table in good repair. If such a table is unavailable, teachers may use a small swimming pool or a large plastic bin, perhaps from Rubbermaid. Child-sized tidy-up materials, such as sponges, a bucket, a mop, and small towels, complement water table use. A small table or shelving unit is needed for storing student materials.

Here are some materials and resources that we have found to be useful in promoting learning at the Water centre:

- containers that have spouts of different shapes for pouring
- containers and plastic bottles of different sizes for measuring, both standard and non-standard form
- basters and eyedroppers of different sizes
- funnels of different sizes
- water wheels, both homemade and commercial
- bottle attachments that create tornadoes
- containers with holes of different sizes at different levels so that the children can experiment with water pressure
- different sizes of tubing, such as plumbers use
- materials to add to the water to change its state (e.g., food coloring, soap, salt, snow, ice)
- kitchen tools (e.g., egg beaters, whisks, spatulas, spoons)
- rocks and other paper weights to observe movement of liquids
- sponges of different sizes, both natural and manufactured
- materials that create waterfalls (e.g., plastic blocks of different heights)
- paper, graph paper, acetate, and plastic clipboards for recording information
- books to provide information about the properties of water and to help inform predictions

---

Books at the Water Centre

Many of the following titles are available in school and public libraries, as well as bookstores. Other titles could be easily substituted and used for the various literacy activities. It is a good idea for teachers to search their school libraries for fiction and non-fiction titles that are related to water, its properties, and the creatures that live in it.

Non-fiction We Found Useful

- *Water* by Brenda Walpole
- *Why Are There Waves?: Questions Children Ask About Water* by Christopher Maynard and Terry Martin
- *My World of Science: Water* by Angela Royston

- *How We Use Water* by Carol Ballard
- *Waters* by Edith Newlin Chase
- *A Cool Drink of Water* by Barbara Kerley
- *Boat Book* by Gail Gibbons
- *Water* by Frank Asch
- *Talk About Water* by Angela Webb

Fiction We Found Helpful

- *Puddles* by Jonathan London (pictures by G. Brian Karas)
- *10 Little Rubber Ducks* by Eric Carle
- *Mister Seahorse* by Eric Carle
- *The Wide-Mouthed Frog* by Keith Faulkner (illustrated by Jonathan Lambert)
- *A Fish Story* by Keith Faulkner (illustrated by Jonathan Lambert)
- *Waiting for the Whales* by Sheryl McFarlane and Ron Lightburn
- *Ten Little Fish* by Audrey Wood (illustrated by Bruce Wood)
- *I Love Boats* by Flora McDonnell
- *Beneath the Bridge* by Hazel Hutchins (illustrated by Ruth Ohi)
- *Mr. Archimedes' Bath* by Pamela Allen
- *Who Sank the Boat?* by Pamela Allen
- *Hooray for Fish* by Lucy Cousins
- *Pop! A Book About Bubbles* by Kimberly Bradley (photographs by Margaret Miller)
- *Mr. Gumpy's Outing* by John Burningham

Literacy Activities in the Water Centre

All the learning at the Water centre can be enriched, supported, and extended through various literacy activities. With the infusion of related texts, charts, games, models, videos, computer activities, authentic artifacts (e.g., seashells and pieces of coral), and authentic materials (e.g., cups and funnels), the Water centre can become an excellent springboard for literacy learning. Activities here can provide the children with many opportunities to expand their vocabulary and explore scientific, mathematical, and dramatic concepts and terms. There are many occasions when the children are encouraged to speak, listen, question, read pictorial and written directions, and record their observations.

Depending on the interest of the children, extensions may last for a few days, a few weeks, or longer. The suggestions outlined below have been successful in stimulating a renewed interest in literacy acquisition. The interests of the children and the teacher as well as the materials available will help determine which literacy activities are selected.

Boats in the water

Plan to introduce this extension during the large-group read-aloud time. We liked to read aloud *I Love Boats* by Flora McDonnell or *Boat Book* by Gail Gibbons. If these books are not available in your library/resource centre, then ask your teacher-librarian for help in finding similar materials. The read-aloud might inspire a discussion about different kinds of boats. Then, during a Shared Writing experience, record on chart paper the kinds of boats the children have heard about, perhaps a sailboat, speedboat, canoe, submarine, cruise ship, and rowboat. Here is an excellent opportunity to demonstrate how print works, for example, left-to-right progression, top-to-bottom flow, and sound–symbol relationship.

Create simple word puzzles. Print in lower case letters the boat words on cards and use either a sticker or an Internet image as the picture for each type of boat. To make the puzzles, cut each card in half, separating the image from the word. In addition, you might provide a selection of photographs of boats and have the children use these resources to match the text on the chart and illustrate it. Be sure to add this chart to the Water centre. Invite the children to bring in toy boats from home for their play.

After the children have had ample opportunity to dramatize with the boats, suggest that they create a marina. Add Popsicle sticks, plastic baskets, stacking rings, or plastic Ping-Pong balls, and any other materials that the children find to make docks, buoys, and dry docks. Try adding string for the children to section off areas of the marina which they might, for example, reserve for gas pumps for the motorboats. After the children have worked with the materials at the marina, invite them to use pictures, numbers, and words to record their work. You might see text like this:

Imabs
for "I made a boathouse."

Creating tornadoes

Children love to watch and discuss water movement, and this fascination can be readily used to develop observation skills and introduce descriptive oral language — "What is the water doing? Is it spinning? swirling? swooshing? rotating? flushing? or gushing?"

Collect various large, plastic pop bottles and attach them in pairs using a small, plastic "tornado maker." These bottle connections can be inexpensively purchased at any science or educational store. The gadgets allow water to shift between the bottles and its movement will resemble that of a tornado.

Plan to add food coloring, sparkles, or sequins to various liquids in different bottles. These variations will stimulate discussion about how the tornadoes are similar and different. Children might say something like "The water in the red bottle is moving faster because I was spinning it so hard" or "The one with the silver sequins looks like a windy day with papers blowing all around."

Stimulate discussion and learning further and extend the play through books and pictures. Collect and read non-fiction books about tornadoes. Search the Internet for photographs of tornadoes and other natural water movements such as waterfalls — you may want to get these laminated. These books and pictures can be added to the Water centre albeit on a shelf or table not "in" the water.

Creating an aquarium

During a read-aloud, share *My Visit to the Aquarium* by Aliki. With its colorful full-page illustrations and lyrical text, the book may well inspire the children to create an aquarium at the Water centre.

Another good way to introduce this extension is to read aloud *A Fish Story* by Keith Faulkner. In this story, the main character finds a small fish and brings it home as a pet. At first, it lives in a small glass bowl and as it grows and grows,

A useful routine to reinforce at the Water centre is for children to dry their hands before they handle any books.

it moves into a bigger bowl, into the bathtub, and finally into the sea, where it is released. Discuss why it was not fair to let the big fish live in the main character's home in a small bowl, and help the children to understand that underwater animals need an appropriate space to live.

While many animals live in the wild, introduce the children to the concept that some animals are captured and live in a public aquarium. Explain to the children that the staff at the aquarium ensures that the animals are safe and also plays an important role in teaching people about the animals. If your school is near an aquarium, a trip to it might be appropriate.

Invite the children to record their knowledge of aquariums to let you assess their prior knowledge. Present individual children or pairs with a large sheet of painting paper on which to draw an aquarium filled with various kinds of fish, coral, and seaweed. Many will know about aquariums because they have small fish tanks or aquariums at home or have seen related shows on television. More advanced literacy learners could later label their pictures, turning their work into a diagram. Oral discussion can stimulate the creation of an aquarium at the Water centre.

Collect plastic models of various sea creatures, including a whale, fish, turtle, snake, jellyfish, octopus, stingray, and shark. Have the children sort these small-scale creatures and store in bins that are labelled. Place the bins at the Water centre. With a small group of children at the Water centre, make a list of all these creatures. Have the children share their work at the Gathering Time and then post the list beside the centre.

Use these new words to create a Bingo game. The words can be written on Bingo game cards, while the matching pictures or photographs can be mounted on the call cards. This format encourages the children to look for initial consonants to make a match and helps them develop some meaningful sight vocabulary. (For more information about how to make and play this game, see Appendix B: Games.)

Find real shells of various shapes and sizes and add them to a labelled pictorial or printed spot at the Water centre. Include pieces of real coral, plastic seaweed, and other items from the fish section in a pet shop. Plastic fencing from a farm set or small plastic blocks might also help to make individual sections for various animals. The children may discuss the importance and need for these divisions. One child might say, "The sharks can't be in the same area as the turtles because they will eat them!"

Studying pond life

Collect books about the pond and things that live in or around the pond. Ask your teacher-librarian to help find good books that are appropriate for children of this age and stage of development. Specifically, non-fiction books about the life cycle of a frog can be very informative. At the large-group time, use this information to create a visual about the stages of a frog's development. Educational stores sell plastic models of frogs at the various stages — egg, tadpole, tadpole with legs, and frog — and these pieces are effective in the water as well as useful when sequencing the stages.

Provide the children with an opportunity to express their scientific knowledge in writing or pictorial form. Have them create a sequencing chart by using long strips of chart paper that have been folded into four sections for the four stages of a frog. The children might like to add an extra section for a title "The Life Cycle of a Frog." (See Appendix A: Ways to Record Ideas for information on how to construct a sequencing, or story, map.)

Plastic models of the various kinds and colors of frogs, as well as of turtles and fish, will transform the Water centre into a pond environment. Add plastic water lilies and lily pads so the animals can float — you can extend the children's imagination by using small plastic plates or bowls as lily pads.

Swimming at the Water centre

A good way to introduce this extension is to teach the children to sing this traditional song:

> Swimming, swimming in the swimming pool,
> When days are hot when days are cold in the swimming pool,
> Breast stroke, side stroke,
> Fancy diving too,
> Oh, don't you wish you never had anything else to do?

Write the lyrics on chart paper so the children can follow along as they sing. Later, post the text in the classroom, or fold and add to the Reading centre so the children can revisit it and use a pointer to identify particular, repeated, or high-frequency words.

Many children love to swim, so consider making the Water centre into a pool where the children can dramatize and act out their experiences, for example: "Last summer, I went to a pool and my dad was using a noodle while I was floating in an inner tube." Add models of people and mini-flotation devices, as well as small plastic diving boards, lounge chairs, and umbrellas. Playmobil or Lego pieces might be very helpful in making this centre come alive.

Finally, the children can use the paper and pencils available at the centre to make signs. Possible signs include Lifeguard on Duty, Swim at your own risk, Pool is closed for cleaning, and Pool Hours. You can help a sign maker by saying the desired word slowly and accentuating each sound as the child writes down the sounds heard (e.g., P . . . oo . . .). Dependent on children's knowledge of sound–symbol relationships, initial consonants, final consonants, and vowels, the teacher would expect such responses as *P*, *Pl*, *Pol*, or *Pool*.

Exploring capacity

Engage the children in collecting plastic containers of various sizes and shapes. Encourage them to search with their parents to find plastic water bottles, pop bottles, vitamin bottles, and other rinsed food containers. This challenge will open a discussion about the importance of reusing and recycling materials, and may lead to an investigation of ways to recycle. Add these materials to the Water centre.

Children love to pour water. Challenge them to fill the containers with scoops of water and then record their results. Ask questions such as these: "Which container took the most scoops to fill?" "Which container took the least number of scoops to fill?" "Let's try to order them from largest to smallest." Provide a simple recording sheet for the children to use either pictorially or written. (For more information on simple recording sheets, see Appendix A: Ways to Record Ideas.)

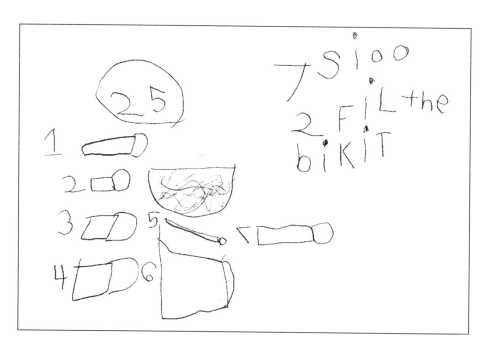

Having predicted it will take 25 scoops to fill a bucket, a child subsequently finds it will take seven. Seven scoops are shown with a caption meaning "7 scoops to fill the bucket."

Children must always be supervised when using plastic bags and containers, so the bag-piercing activity would be an appropriate one for a classroom assistant or parent volunteer to oversee.

One property of water is that it takes the shape of its container. Teachers can explore this fact with the children by adding less traditional containers to the Water centre. Large and small Ziploc bags, balloons, rubber gloves, and watering cans can demonstrate the ways that water can move. Once a container is filled, consider poking a small hole in the bottom and having the children watch the water pour, drip, or flow out. Develop oral language skills by asking, "How does the water move differently when the hole is larger?"

Work with a small group of children to record the results when these different containers are filled. Take photographs of the bags and gloves when they are empty and full, and use these images to make a lift-the-flap book called "Empty and Full."

Rainbow of Bottles

Invite the children to bring empty water bottles to school and use this collection to create a display. Have the children sort the bottles by size to find the bottles that are all the same size; then, have them work in pairs to use a funnel to fill each bottle with water. Add a few drops of food coloring to each bottle and mix. Encourage the children to make oral predictions about the results. For example, a child might say, "If I add a drop of yellow and a drop of red, the water will turn to orange." Attempt to make various shades of each color and ask what might happen if you add more drops of the same color. For example, a child might observe, "One drop of blue is light blue, but five drops is much darker." Try sorting the bottles by color and placing them on a windowsill for an impressive water display. Invite the children to draw the Rainbow of Bottles or to record their investigation in pictures or words. For example, a child might make a blue mark with a blue marker, a red mark with a red marker and then a purple mark to show what happened when he was experimenting. More advanced writers might use letters or words to record their findings, for example,

blo + rd = purple
for "blue + red = purple"

Red and yellow and pink and green,
Purple and orange and blue,
I can sing a rainbow,
Sing a rainbow,
Sing a rainbow too!

Collect fiction and non-fiction books about colors and rainbows and teach the "I Can Sing a Rainbow" song by Arthur Hamilton (lyrics at left). Write these lyrics on chart paper, printing the color words in the appropriate color. Extend this Shared Reading activity by writing individual sentence strips and challenging the children to reread the lines and reassemble the song. A large pocket chart can be useful. When the children become proficient at meeting this challenge, make it more difficult by cutting the sentences into individual words to reassemble.

Soap in the water

At the Gathering Time, read aloud *Malcolm's Runaway Soap* by Jo Ellen Bogart and invite the children to bring in the wrappers or labels of soaps they use at home.

To develop visual discrimination and oral language, as well as beginning reading skills, make a matching or Concentration game with two of each wrapper or label, for example, Dove, Ivory, Tide, Cascade, Dawn, and Palmolive. Store the game in a plastic Ziploc bag at the Water centre. After the children have enjoyed the game, you might collate these pieces of environmental print into a class book and read it with the class in a Shared Reading session. You could later add the book to the Reading centre for the children's use during the activity period.

Have a large- or small-group discussion about the various kinds of soaps available, for example, flakes, bars, and liquids. Brainstorm with the children the various uses of soap, namely, to wash one's body, wash clothes, wash dishes, clean a dog, and clean a car. Use this information to make a class book, "Uses of Soap."

To prompt some inquiries, collect different bars of soap — hotel soaps and small gift soaps can offer variation. At the Water centre, discuss their similarities and differences in size, shape, color, smell, and texture, for example, and then place them in the water to test their buoyancy. Make a chart to indicate which bars sank and which ones floated (see Appendix A: Ways to Record Ideas). Talk about the clarity of the water before and after the soap suds were added. "At first, I could see through the water and then it was all cloudy." Invite the small group of children who did this activity to share their work at the Celebration time at the end of the activity period. This soap activity would be repeated over the course of a week with different children.

Playing with bubbles

Bubbles

Dip the wand and gently blow,
Watch the tiny bubbles grow,
Big and bigger,
Round and fat,
Rainbow colored,
And then splat!

Begin by chanting the poem "Bubbles" (at left) or by reading *Pop! A Book About Bubbles* by Kimberly Bradley, a simple text that provides explanations about how bubbles are formed and why they pop. Another book that has proven successful is *Bubble Trouble* by Margaret Mahy. This is the story of a girl named Mabel whose little brother gets trapped inside her big bubble and floats all around the town.

Invite the children to bring in different kinds of liquid detergents, commercial bubble mix, and bubble bath products for experimentation, making and blowing bubbles. Provide the children with materials to make bubble wands — for example, pipe cleaners, plastic berry baskets, and wire — and large pie plates to hold the bubble mix. In addition, provide commercial wands of varying sizes and shapes. All of these resources will be kept at the Water centre. Be sure to do this bubble-blowing activity during outdoor play.

What happened at the Water centre?

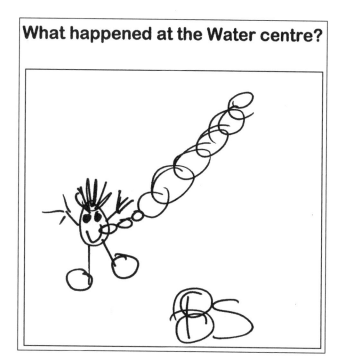

After a child, Devon, illustrated his response to the question, he was asked to describe what he had done. "I made bubbles at the Water centre today," he reported.

The following bubble recipes have proven to be very successful. Try to take this opportunity to follow a recipe with the children. Consider printing your favorite bubble recipe on waterproof cards for the children to independently use later to practise their reading skills.

Bubble Recipes

2 cups / 500 ml warm water
6 tablespoons glycerin (from drugstore)
6 tablespoons liquid detergent (Dawn, not ultra)
dash of sugar
or
2 cups / 500 ml distilled water
1/2 cup / 125 ml Blue Dawn detergent
1/4 cup / 60 ml light corn syrup
Be careful to avoid foam by mixing slowly.
Place in a sealed container overnight.

To make jumbo bubbles, use this recipe from *Toad Cottages and Shooting Stars* by Sharon Lovejoy:
6 cups / 1.5 L water
2 cups / 500 ml Blue Dawn
1 cup / 250 ml corn syrup
Mix the above ingredients and store overnight in a sealed plastic container.

Provide the children with lots of time to report to the group as to which wands and bubble mixtures worked best.

A child named Emily commented, "Science is trees and flowers and snakes and rocks and dinosaurs so I made them all on the front of 'My Science Book.'"

Recording ideas

All of these activities at the Water centre are valuable and generate ideas for recording. Sometimes children share their learning orally by retelling the events with the teacher or the whole class during large-group Gathering Times. Teachers may also capture the learning with a photograph. Some children might use illustrations to record their work in the water, while other more advanced literacy learners might use pictures, numbers, labels, or full sentences to record their efforts. Provide the children with "Science books" to gather photographs and record their work in the Water centre (and the Sand centre). This recording book could be 10 blank sheets of 8 1/2 by 11 inch paper with a construction paper cover. Have the children design a cover by printing their name and drawing items related to the interest, for example, sea creatures, shovels, waves, and boats.

Creating an Environment for Success in the Water Centre

The following section is presented in terms of questions that the reflective practitioner is encouraged to ask about the classroom's Water centre. The answers reflect what we have found to be best practices.

1. How do I ensure that the Water centre is safe?

- Introduce the children to the routines and expectations for the centre. For example, they should mop regularly to reduce slippage.
- Change the water daily. Enlist the help of students in the upper grades to do this.
- Keep the temperature of the water comfortable.
- Regularly wash the equipment with a mild, eco-friendly soap.
- Regularly check the materials for breakage or damage.
- Consider health issues when adding any equipment. For example, be sure to remind the children not to put any equipment in their mouths or to drink the water.
- Discuss with the children how many of them can safely use this centre. (No more than three is recommended.)
- Post a picture or print a sign indicating the number of children who can safely play.
- Ensure that the water table is within your hearing and sight or that of another adult.

2. How do I ensure that tidy up is successful and that the children take responsibility for it?

- When introducing new equipment, trace each item on a table or shelf for easy tidy up.
- Put tools that are no longer being used in labelled bins or baskets for future use.
- Arrange the storage containers on marked shelves or on a table near the water table.
- Introduce and remove the materials as necessary to avoid clutter and disorganization.

- Establish clear expectations for cleanup. For example, you will want the children to return the materials to the correct labelled spots and mop up any water on the floor.
- Provide a good child-sized mop for soaking up any water spilled accidentally.
- Give the children at the Water centre a five-minute head start since they may take longer to complete their tidy up.
- Add the five plastic letters W A T E R to the Water centre, and have the children spell the word in the water to indicate when all the materials are tidy.

3. What is my role as a teacher at the Water centre?

- Introduce the Water centre through a Shared Reading experience. Read a book, poem, or song, for example, "Row, Row, Row, Your Boat."
- Gradually introduce any new materials or routines to the whole group.
- Ensure that this centre is exciting and vibrant. Add surprises. For example, change the color of the water to stimulate discussion, fill the Water table with snow, or add dish detergent to make bubbles in the water.
- Plan for specific literacy learning to occur. As one example, read a favorite alphabet book and work with the children to create a class alphabet book about the various creatures that live in the water (e.g., A – Alligator, B – Beluga whale, C – Crab).
- When deciding on a literacy extension, remember to listen to the children and follow their interest. If many of the children are talking about their cottage, vacation, or trip to a city waterfront, for example, then a marina extension with boats might be suitable for the Water centre.
- Be sure to develop a schedule for observing a manageable number of children as they work at the Water centre.
- Encourage the children to retell, relate, and reflect on their play in the water as well as use pictures, numbers, and words to record their work at this centre. (At left is a child's text for "I found 5 tadpoles.")
- Twin children of different stages to ensure language development and investigation.
- Regularly introduce materials/equipment that can motivate or help the children solve their inquiries.
- Maintain health standards by changing the water daily and consider having the children fill the water table some of the time, predicting and recording how many buckets are needed to fill it.
- Direct children to their peers for information and help.

4. How might I ensure that the children and their parents/guardians value the Water centre as much as the Reading centre and the Drawing/Writing centre?

- Timetable the centre so that it is part of a Math, Science, and Technology activity period.
- Be sure to have the Water centre inside the Kindergarten classroom. Despite space constraints, resist having it in the hallway because that diminishes its importance and makes it difficult to monitor and extend the learning.
- Schedule adult time at the centre so that you, a student teacher, an educational assistant, or a parent volunteer can observe and interact with the children, answering questions, posing new questions, and extending the learning.

- Share important discoveries with the class at large-group times. For example, have the children tell how many buckets it took to fill the water table. The amount will often change as it is dependent on how accurate the measurement is and how high the children fill the table.
- Include photographs and simple recordings of the children's work in portfolios for reporting to parents. These folders, each showing the name of the child on the front, will also contain dated samples of work that reflect student progress.
- Make a class booklet of photographs with captions of the specific concepts that the children are learning in the Water centre.
- In a newsletter, inform parents about the importance of the learning with the water. Show children's work samples that reflect a range of expertise. For example, one sample might relate to a child filling and emptying a bottle of water while another might focus on a child filling up a series of bottles and arranging them by size.
- Hold a Parents' Night to share the purpose of the centre and outline the range of learning that occurs. For example, point out the range of skills from simply pouring to ordering containers according to volume and recording the results. Consider charting some of the developmental mileposts at the Water centre for parents' reference.

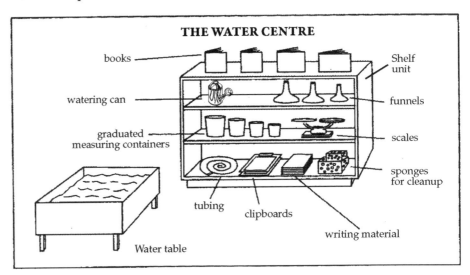

THE WATER CENTRE

books — Shelf unit

watering can — funnels

graduated measuring containers — scales

tubing — clipboards

writing material

sponges for cleanup

Water table

Exploring the many forms of water, from bubbles to snow, at the Water centre gives children many interesting topics to talk and write about.

Mileposts to Help Guide Teacher Observations of Children Working with Water

These developmental mileposts are guidelines only — they are not intended to be all-inclusive or prescriptive; they can, however, be tremendously informative in guiding teacher interaction with children and in planning for extensions. They can also be treated as a quick checklist when preparing for parent–teacher interviews. A quick way to record observations is to photocopy a set of these mileposts for each child, and date, check, or circle the points that apply to individual students. We recommend using a different color of pen for each term.

How children show an interest in the water

Children interested in water voluntarily choose water as an activity. They willingly experiment and explore the properties of water, using a variety of tools. They can concentrate for a reasonable time. They willingly take risks, perhaps saying, "Let's see what happens when we add salt to the water." Children accept responsibility for their own behaviors. They might also show leadership by helping other children to solve problems or tidy up.

How children approach play with water

Over time, children will become more involved in water play and in their relations with other children. As they become more socially mature, they tend to move through the different kinds of play according to their interests. For example, on one day a child might prefer to work alone filling bottles and the next day, the same child might choose to work co-operatively to play a matching game. Typical milestones are identified below:

- working alone (solitary play)
- working side by side with other children, making own structure with own equipment (parallel play)
- working co-operatively, sharing and taking turns, and exchanging ideas with other children (co-operative play)

Literacy skills that children demonstrate in the Water centre

There are many literacy skills that children might demonstrate.

- Children use oral language to label, describe, retell, relate, question, and report observations and experiences in the water.
- They talk about the ideas that the materials provided and discuss what they are doing with the water.
- Children listen to teacher comments about the play. For example, if the teacher says, "I see that you have made a dock," the child might respond, "Yes, I have. I saw one at the island when I went there with my granny."
- Children retell, relate, or make a connection in their world. For example, a child says, "When I stick my hand in this bucket, the water goes up and pours out. That's just like at home in my bathtub. I have to be careful not to make the water go all over the floor."
- They refer to books, photographs, videos, and the Internet for information and ideas to inform the play.
- They use signs that were generated at a Shared Writing time to label their work.
- They make signs of their own to label their work, for example, motorboat, sailboat, dock.
- Children write narrative or expository text to describe their work and retell what they did.

    I T 4 S T FL D K.

    for "I took 4 scoops to fill the cup."
- Children record discoveries and results of simple experiments. The teacher might challenge the children to record what happens when they mix water with other materials (e.g., salt, sugar, oil, or sand). (See Appendix A: Ways to Record Ideas.)

- Children apply new knowledge to other situations. Perhaps the children have been following a recipe for cookies where accurate measurements were necessary. In the Water centre they might apply this new learning by pouring water more carefully and using standard measures (e.g., measuring spoons, cups, and litre pitchers).

Other skills that children demonstrate

Children might do any of the following:

- feeling the water, letting it run through their fingers, moving the water, splashing it
- dragging their hands through the water; patting the water to make different splashes
- moving objects through and under the water and from one container to another
- using other materials to move the water (e.g., funnels, spoons, scoops, and basters)
- filling containers with increasing control and accuracy and recognizing quantities of water: more, less, same
- using non-standard materials to compare quantity (e.g., containers of different sizes) and then using standardized materials to measure (e.g., graduated containers, simple scales, and measuring spoons)
- adding materials to water to change its feel and look (e.g., soap, salt, oil)
- under adult supervision, changing the properties of water — for example, heating it, freezing it, thawing it

Knowledge that children demonstrate

Knowledge that children might demonstrate includes the following:

- using appropriate props in the water to support dramatic play, perhaps adding sea creatures and people as they role-play
- recognizing how water and its properties can be changed with the addition of different materials (For example, a child discovers that salt makes the water more buoyant.)
- recognizing the possibilities for the uses of different tools (e.g., water wheel, funnel)
- using appropriate language to describe, question, predict, estimate, direct, compare, and draw conclusions
- exploring and using new language skills and concepts (For example, a child describes the different colors made with food coloring.)
- exploring and using new mathematical and scientific concepts and skills (e.g., volume, flotation, displacement, and water pressure)

We have come to understand the value of the Water centre in the development of literacy skills. Introducing meaningful, relevant, and stimulating materials to this centre will generate interest and opportunities for children to talk, listen, read, and write.

9

The Construction Centre

Children naturally use readily available materials to build. Even toddlers intuitively manipulate, stack, and sort cardboard boxes, lids, pots, plastic containers, and nesting toys. Teachers can use this natural interest and experience to help bridge the transition between home and school. The introduction of particular materials, both "found" and commercial, can lead children to communicate, consolidate learning, and expand their knowledge and problem-solving abilities.

Construction materials also provide an excellent vehicle for children to acquire and use language. As they build, children have many opportunities to speak, listen, read, write, view, describe, retell, represent, report, question, and resolve conflicts. They are also exposed to specific mathematical, scientific, and technological ideas, for example: "This big, blue block is equal to two small yellow blocks." "This floor area is bigger than that floor area." Working with many commercial and found materials leads children to instinctively create, imagine, dramatize, and express themselves. They learn to represent their ideas using symbols for the real object. For example, a long, thin block becomes a bridge.

Construction materials can be used by children at a variety of ages, stages, and developmental levels. There is no one way to use them, and all children can meet with some success. As a result, the learning experience is non-threatening and invites children to take risks. It thereby builds self-confidence and develops self-esteem. The materials allow children to work independently or in co-operation with others. Social skills, such as sharing, interacting with others, and working co-operatively, are developed. The unique nature of the materials also ensures that important physical skills, such as eye-hand coordination, balance, and large- and small-muscle control, are developed naturally.

Children constantly see different ways of using the materials. Some children simply explore the construction materials and then orally share information about their structure, perhaps talking with a teacher or another child to describe their building and its size, shape, or number of pieces. Other more sophisticated learners might make a plan and then test a simple hypothesis. For example, a child announces, "I am going to build two castles with a bridge in the middle and I think that I can make them three floors tall." Those children who are capable can use a "Structures Booklet" to draw or write about their constructions. This booklet could be several, blank pages stapled together with a construction paper cover.

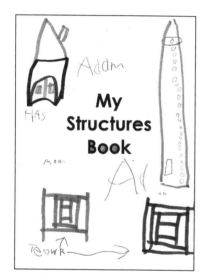

A child named Adam records the things he builds. About the cover of his booklet, he said, "I put the CN Tower and my house on the front. I even made two towers" (taking a bird's eye view).

How to Use a "Structures Booklet"

In a "Structures Booklet," the children might do any of the following:
- draw a picture of their work
- label a photograph

- use symbols to represent a pattern, balance, geometric shapes or measurement, for example: □ ○ □ ○
- count and write down the number of blocks they used
- measure the height or width using non-standard units, for example, determining that a structure is "five hands tall"
- write about what they built and how they did it
- record a plan for what they intend to build

This experience of recording is exciting and stimulating, and can be shared with others and referenced, to show progress. In such an atmosphere, children naturally imitate, question, seek help, and share results, and the teacher has many opportunities to demonstrate new learning.

Rather than having the children complete a page of simple addition facts or a list of numerals, we recommend giving them a simple tally sheet or large graph paper to record how many blocks they use in their structures or in the patterns they make in their buildings. For example, a girl named Paige recorded numbers of colored pieces used in her "Structures Booklet" and said: "I used 21 blue pieces. I used 52 red pieces. I used 40 green pieces. I used 62 yellow pieces." We found that when children were encouraged to record this kind of information, they saw a real need for the learning, took ownership of the task, and became actively engaged. These recording experiences also gave them real, meaningful practice with numbers and numeracy skills.

Giving the children opportunities to share these recordings in front of the class during large-group times is also worthwhile. These mini-oral presentations help children develop language confidence, as well as tone, volume, and voice when speaking to a large group.

Introducing the Construction Centre

Reading a piece of children's literature such as *I Can Build a House* by Shigeo Watanabe or *Building a House* by Byron Barton is a good way to introduce this centre to the whole group. After the reading, we would introduce the materials and demonstrate the routines for constructing and deconstructing. Key routines include carrying a bin with two hands, working on flat surfaces with the exception of the big blocks, and building carefully and quietly.

Once the children have had many opportunities to manipulate the materials and are familiar with the routines, the teacher can extend the activity to include a literacy experience. Through a brainstorm and Shared Writing experience, for example, the class could record buildings that are in the environment (e.g., house, apartment building, skyscraper, mall). We recommend displaying this chart where the construction materials are stored. The children find such a chart useful if they need a resource to help label a structure they have built.

Building activities need to be timetabled as part of the Math, Science, and Technology activity time. During this period, we typically had the Sand centre, the Water centre, the Construction centre, the computer, and math and science games open, while all other classroom centres were closed.

Ways to indicate that a centre is open include use of a sign with the word *Open* on it or a sign in the color green. A sign with the word *Closed* on it or a sign in the color red signifies a closed centre. Children can produce the signs.

Before the children tidy up, invite them to go on a walkabout to view one another's efforts. Individual children will be encouraged to talk about their work, to describe the process they used, the problems they encountered, and the solutions they found. This time helps the children to develop their listening and speaking skills, confidence, and ability to offer ideas and feedback to their peers.

Materials That Encourage Literacy Learning at the Construction Centre

Certain materials in the environment lend themselves to the development of mathematical, scientific, and technological language and concepts. Teachers need to collect a wide range of stackable materials of uniform size and shape to help foster this development. The children and parents can also collect and bring in "found" and recycled materials. These materials should be stored in individually labelled containers, for example, baskets or bins. To ensure choice and variety, it is important to have a large number of construction materials available.

The following recycled or "found" materials have proven successful:

- corks, yarn spools
- beer bungs, both plain and colored
- lipstick lids and lids from other containers
- separate collections of small, medium, and large plastic cups
- cardboard boxes of the same size
- margarine and yogurt containers of the same size
- small plastic bottles of the same size
- egg cartons of the same kind and size

Teachers need to observe their children carefully to determine which materials might be added to encourage further exploration. Some commercial materials lend themselves to the development of particular skills.

- Pattern blocks, Tower-ifics, Unifix cubes, and colored tiles promote the development of patterning concepts.
- Base ten blocks, Unifix cubes, corks, and bungs invite the exploration of number, perimeter, area, and balance.
- Polydron geometric shapes and other geometric shapes help to motivate children to explore geometry.
- Kapla blocks, spools, Unifix blocks, and Cuisenaire rods are examples of materials that help children to experiment with measurement.

All of these concepts are developed by the process of building and then listening, describing, questioning, demonstrating, and recording the work. As we circulated, we promoted this by talking with the children about their structures and using the language of mathematics and science in our responses. For example, one of us might say: "I see that you have covered the whole table with the Kapla blocks. That means you have covered the *area* of your table."

Here are some examples of successful commercial materials:

plain and colored blocks (large and small)	Polydron shapes Tower-ifics

pattern blocks	Bristle blocks
base ten blocks	polygons
Cuisenaire rods	struts
Kapla	geometric shapes, 2D and 3D
Duplo	Unifix blocks
Lego	

After the children have had much experience handling and experimenting with the materials, adding props stimulated further discussion, dramatization, and the subsequent use of written language. Here are examples of props that have been successfully used for constructions:

- miniature counters, cars, trucks, farm and zoo animals, teddy bears, people, and coins
- "found" materials, such as stones, pine cones, shells, twigs, feathers, and bottle caps
- colored disks

Invite the children to use such props after their structures are complete.

It is also important to introduce books and other media about construction. Such materials can be used by the children as a guide to their building or as a reference for captions about their work.

Books About Building

Titles we have read aloud and displayed include the following.

Useful Non-fiction Books

- *How a House Is Built* by Gail Gibbons
- *The House I'll Build for the Wrens* by Shirley Neitzel
- *Let's Go Home. The Wonderful Things About a House* by Cynthia Rylant (illustrated by Wendy Anderson Halperin)
- *Houses and Homes* by Ann Morris (illustrated by Ken Heyman)
- *Building a House* by Byron Barton

Helpful Fiction Titles

- *The Three Pigs: An Architectural Tale* by Steven Guarnaccia
- *Architect of the Moon* by Tim Wynne-Jones

Literacy Activities in the Construction Centre

Building with construction materials provides children with countless opportunities to develop competence in the area of language development and literacy. Children see real purposes for listening, speaking, viewing, reading, and writing. Through the Construction centre, the teacher can demonstrate and model written language and read aloud fiction and non-fiction to develop children's listening and oral vocabulary, as well as motivate the children to become readers and writers.

In a school year, a Kindergarten classroom would not explore all of the literacy ideas and activities listed and outlined below; instead, the teacher would select the ones most relevant to the interests and abilities of the learners. Some activities might include all of the children and last for several weeks. Other challenges might last for one or two activity periods or large-group times.

Talking about building

Many topics are related to construction and building. One-on-one while the children are building or during large-group Gathering Times, the teacher and children might discuss the following:

- types of buildings (e.g., towers, houses, pyramids, castles)
- other structures in the environment (e.g., bridges, dams, subways, roads, apartments, monuments, walls, dams, canals, silos)
- famous buildings or structures (e.g., Eiffel Tower, CN Tower)
- construction site material (e.g., wood, stone, concrete, cement, steel)
- tools (e.g., hammers, saws)
- machines (e.g., diggers, bulldozers, cranes, excavators)
- construction workers (e.g., carpenters, laborers, welders)

Any of these discussions could be recorded in chart or word web format.

Focusing on famous structures

The Construction centre provides the impetus for a homework activity where the children talk with their family members about famous buildings and structures such as the pyramids, CN Tower, and Great Wall of China. Suggest that families search for postcards, photographs, and magazine pictures of these structures. They could perhaps obtain travel agency brochures that feature some of the structures. The images can then be added to the Construction centre for visual reference as the children build. When interest wanes, the children can place the images into a booklet and label them. The booklet can later be added to the Reading centre for reference.

Making a construction site visit

Prepare the children for a visit to a real construction site by writing them a Daily Message (see Chapter 2). The invitation to go for a walk to look at the local site might read like this:

> Dear Children,
>
> Today we are going to go for a walk to see a new building being built at the end of our street.
>
> What do you think we will see?
>
> From,
>
> Mrs. Green

At a Shared Reading time, point to the words and have the children orally share their ideas; then, take them to a neighborhood construction site. (Make sure any appropriate permission slips have been completed.) From safely behind the hoarding, they will be able to view the activities of the construction workers. Remember to take photographs to record the visit. Back in the Kindergarten classroom, discuss the sights and sounds at the site. In a Shared Writing

In conversation with the teacher, a child said, "The house that I built is almost as tall as me." Her record reflects that.

experience, list the children's ideas. Ask a few children to mount the photographs on cardboard and create hand-printed labels on construction paper. You might see

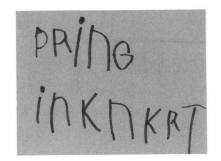

This child-produced sign means "Pouring in Concrete."

Have a small group present this board to the class and then display it at the Construction centre.

From real tools to dramatic props

Invite a construction worker — for example, a carpenter or plumber — to visit the Kindergarten to describe what he or she does. Ask the worker to bring some tools to show the children and to be prepared to answer questions. Twenty to 30 minutes is a good visit length. After the visit, with help from the children's families, collect props, such as safety vests, hard hats, work gloves, pylons, measuring tapes, clipboards, architectural plans, and flags. Add them to the Construction centre to be used with the big blocks. As the children begin to dramatize with these props, suggest that they print signs to use with their structures, for example, Stop, Yield, Danger, No Entry. It is also a good idea to introduce them to the colors and shapes of common signs by showing pictures of signs printed from the Internet.

Designing houses for the three pigs

Introduce the children to the job of architect by reading *The Three Pigs: An Architectural Tale* by Steven Guarnaccia. This child-friendly, informative book entertains Kindergartners as it introduces them to the world of architecture and design. It cleverly retells the fairy tale as famous architects design the houses for the three pigs. It exposes the children to the process of designing and building a house, and includes related materials such as plans and a drafting board. The book's endpapers extend vocabulary by introducing all the tools that an architect might use. Through this text, the children may develop an interest in creating their own plans in oral, pictorial, or written form.

Construction tools game

One way to prepare children for the game is to read *The House I'll Build for the Wrens* by Shirley Neitzel. This book, in repetitive, cumulative text, cleverly introduces many construction tools. Use stickers or illustrations to make a card game modelled on Go Fish: you will need two sets of cards featuring pictures of tools, for example, a hammer, a saw, a metre-stick, a nail, a screwdriver, a wheelbarrow, a traffic sign, and a screw. Help the children at the centre to ask each other questions: "Do you have a screwdriver?" "Do you have a wheelbarrow?" This game is tremendously encouraging for young children learning to formulate questions. A good book to extend this interest is *The Toolbox* by Anne Rockwell.

Machines and vehicles: Constructing words

Begin by reading non-fiction books about machines. Some books we have used successfully are *Truck* by Donald Crews, *Big Book of Construction Machines* (John Deere series), *Machines at Work* by Byron Barton, and *The Construction Alphabet Book* by Jerry Pallotta. Remember to check with your teacher-librarian to find suitable videos and CDs that might be available for viewing. Add models of machines that the children might have seen at a neighborhood construction site or in a book (e.g., bulldozer, dump truck). Encourage families to view, if possible, the Treehouse channel program *Big Machines*. After creating a list of these machines at a large-group time, use magnetic letters to spell their names on cards by tracing around each plastic letter. (Choose magnetic letters in a clean standard font with upper and lower case variations.) At activity time, the children might complete these puzzles by finding the appropriate letters and reconstructing the words.

Lunchbox games

Be sure to have the children name the food items. You might invite one child to unpack the lunchbox in the middle of the circle. It can also be a child who removes an item and hides it behind his or her back.

Collect models of food from the Home/Dramatic Play centre and add them to a lunchbox for a construction worker. After the children have had some time to explore the items, gather them in a circle. Display the items. To develop visual discrimination and visual memory, prompt the children to close their eyes, remove one item, and then ask, "What item from the construction worker's lunch is missing?" We like to play this game over several days with the same five items. The game could be extended by changing these familiar items, and as the children meet with success, the number of items can increase to 10.

The food item–filled lunchbox can also be used to develop auditory memory. Whisper a sentence like this to the first child in the circle: "The construction worker had *a turkey sandwich* in his lunchbox." In turn, each child whispers the beginning of the sentence, repeating the previous item(s) in order, and then adds a new item for the next child in the circle to remember. For example: "The construction worker had a turkey sandwich and *an apple* in his lunchbox." A similar game can be created with a worker's tools, using photographs, pictures, or real and plastic tools.

Making bridges

Create an environment that encourages the children to think and talk about bridges. You can collect picture books that depict bridges and add them to the Construction centre. You might read a version of "Three Billy Goats Gruff" to stimulate an interest in different kinds of bridges, such as suspension bridge, drawbridge, pylon bridge, and trestle bridge. Search the Internet for bridge images and pictures of famous bridges, such as the Confederation Bridge between Prince Edward Island and New Brunswick and the Golden Gate Bridge in San Francisco. If possible, project the images on a SMART Board so everyone can easily view and discuss them. Add rulers, metre-sticks, planks, and boards to the Construction centre so that children can use these resources and the information provided to build their own bridges.

Setting up a fire station

Share the following "Fire Station" song, writing it on chart paper to encourage the children to add actions and follow along.

Ding! Ding! Ding! Ding!
Hear the sirens blowing,
Ding! Ding! Ding! Ding!
Everybody's going,
Climb the ladder,
Point the hose,
With a whoosh, whoosh, whoosh,
Out the fire goes!

Visit a local fire station or invite a firefighter to visit the class.

Collect dress-up materials that could help the Construction centre become a fire station. These materials include hats, uniforms, and badges. The children can use the big blocks to create a fire station and then use recycled and "found" materials to make a fire hydrant. Add a short water hose or plastic tubing to the hydrant so that the children can dramatize putting out large fires. Be sure to include several telephones at the centre so that the children can make and respond to emergency calls: "911. What is your emergency?" Notepads can be an effective way to record information about the caller's address and any emergency situation.

Let's create a circus!

It can be effective to challenge the children to transform the big blocks area within the Construction centre into a circus. You may want to introduce and promote the idea by reading aloud *Peter Spier's Circus*. After the large-group read-aloud, plan to use this beautifully illustrated book for a picture study with a small group, where all the children in the group can see the illustrations of marvellous circus acts and performers. *Peter Spier's Circus* presents an excellent opportunity for children to develop descriptive oral vocabulary as they comment on what they see at the circus.

Either in the large group or in a small group, make a list of circus items and add illustrations as cues. Post the chart of items beside the big blocks in the Construction centre for the children to refer to and read as they build. Inspire the children by adding hula hoops, large metre-sticks, and stuffed animals such as elephants and tigers. Children will use these materials along with the various sizes of blocks to create a circus atmosphere.

Building on Interest in Circuses

A circus setup in the Construction centre can elicit an interest in circuses that opens up many opportunities for literacy learning.

Circus Performers: Build on interest in the circus by sharing Ian Falconer's *Olivia Saves the Circus* in a read-aloud session. After you have read about all the sick performers and how Olivia the pig saves the day, on a chart or whiteboard, list all the performers that the children can recall from the story, for example, juggler, tightrope walker, lion tamer, and clowns — the illustrations on the four-page fold-out are most helpful in supporting this recall. A small group at the Drawing/Writing centre may want to make illustrations of various performers and provide captions about them; these can then be assembled into a "Circus Book."

Another idea is to let children match cards that feature performers with cards that show their props or equipment — for example, dog and hoop, magician and magic wand, lion tamer and whip, acrobat and trapeze, seal and ball. Children can work alone or with a partner to find the matching pairs among the face-down cards.

Animals in the Circus: Generate interest by reading aloud *The Circus Ship* by Chris Van Dusen during a large-group session. In this rhyming text, a circus ship is shipwrecked and all the animals are saved.

You can then capitalize on the children's interest and new knowledge by encouraging them to play a game modelled on Go Fish — children will gain an opportunity to use new vocabulary and develop their skill in asking questions. Place stickers or pictures of circus animals on blank playing cards. Each player receives six cards and, in turn, asks a partner a question such as, "Do you have a lion?" If the partner has a lion, he or she passes the card to the questioning player, and the matching pair of cards is placed to the side. The questioning player asks for other circus animals until no more matches can be made. If the partner does not have the appropriate card, the player says, "Go to the circus," and the first player picks up from the deck. The partner then requests an animal and so on until all of one player's cards are gone. The player with the most pairs at the end of the game is the winner.

From Large-Scale Building to Dioramas: Using a cardboard box for the setting, interested children can work individually or in small groups at the Visual Arts centre to create a small-scale circus. They can paint or cut and paste the background and use models to depict the circus. Playmobil circus models or small plastic animals are excellent for supporting dramatic play and language development.

Circus Bingo: Making two sets of cards, one with pictures of circus acts or performers and one with pictures and words for the caller to use, is a worthwhile extension. This game challenges the caller to read either the pictures or the words. The chart in the big blocks area (see "Let's create a circus!," previous page) will serve as a helpful reference. Appendix B: Games provides instructions on how to play Bingo.

Dressing the Clown: With the children in a large group, brainstorm all the items of clothing that a clown might wear — big glasses, funny nose, oversized shoes, baggy pants, and large bow tie. Record the items identified and then make a felt-board clown with a variety of cut-out clothes. The children can then assemble the clown individually or in pairs, taking turns adding an item of clothing. This dressing activity provides a great opportunity for the acquisition of new vocabulary and oral expression.

Holding a Circus Day: If interest in circus activities persists after several weeks, you may want to work with parent volunteers or older students, as well as the physical education instructor, to hold a Circus Day. This event could take place in the gym, in the classroom, or even in a hallway. In preparation, the children might make signs, draw posters, and write invitations. Typical featured activities include tightrope walking along a bench; juggling with hoops, balls, or plastic bowling pins; face painting; running a popcorn stand; and performing magic tricks. These work best as stations that the children visit on a rotation basis.

To extend any of the games, invite the children to record who played the game and how many pairs of cards each player collected. They could record this information in their Drawing/Writing books and accompany it with an illustration of playing the game.

Some children may choose to use their Drawing/Writing books to draw a picture of the clown and label it.

Castles, dragons, and knights

Knights in Shining Armor by Gail Gibbons uses beautiful watercolor and ink illustrations and labels to introduce the children to the parts of a castle. In a Shared Writing session, label a diagram of a castle, introducing vocabulary such as *drawbridge*, *turret*, *tower*, and *moat*. *Castle* by Christopher Gravett (Eyewitness Books) and *Castle* by Richard Platt (DK Experience) are excellent for stimulating oral vocabulary and expression, as the children view the illustrations in small groups.

Conduct an Internet search and collect pictures of many famous castles and palaces. Post these pictures in the big blocks area of the Construction centre.

After building a tower at the Construction centre, a child has recorded it in a "Structures Booklet" with a prominent label.

Teachers might also provide a large refrigerator box which the children could transform into a castle at the Visual Arts centre.

Here a child has drawn a tower and a castle after building them at the centre. Note the printing of "TR" and "CSL."

At the Construction centre, encourage the children to build castles using the big blocks, as well as the small blocks and other construction materials. Add props, such as flags and shields, and wooden rulers for use as planks. Provide small pieces of construction paper and cardboard, and masking tape so the children can make windows as well as stone patterns and designs on the castle walls and turrets.

People at a Castle: During a read-aloud, share *A Medieval Feast* by Aliki and then, with the children, make a list of all the people who live in a castle — king, queen, knights, court jesters, princesses, princes, and servants. In a small group, some children might choose to create castle-shaped books, drawing one person on each page and following a sentence pattern: "A _____ lives in a castle."

Medieval Feast: If the children show much interest in castles, dragons, and knights, you may want to involve parent volunteers to create a medieval feast complete with food and entertainment. The planning for such an event provides the impetus for many Shared Writing activities and opportunities for literacy development. Children can create invitations, placemats, signs, and banners. Holding a feast also requires devising costumes, scheduling activities, developing entertainment, and preparing food.

Dragon Habitat: The popular song "Puff the Magic Dragon" by Peter Yarrow is available as both a book and as a CD. Reading and singing it can generate great interest in building habitats for dragons — and encourage the teacher to introduce literacy into the big blocks building at the Construction centre. Constructing with both big blocks and small building materials (Duplo) provides the children with many opportunities to imagine, talk, read, write, and view.

Two other books about dragons would also be valuable additions to the centre. *Sleeping Dragons All Around* by Sheree Fitch is a delightful tongue-twisting collection of poems about a little girl and how she deals with her fear of seven strange dragons. The teacher could make a list of all the dragon names, and the children could chant the familiar refrain "I must tiptoe, tiptoe softly as I pass." *The Knight and the Dragon* by Tomie dePaola has almost no words and is therefore easy to read.

Knights: During a large-group read-aloud, read *Knights in Shining Armor* by Gail Gibbons in order to provide the children with an ideal overview of knighthood. Alternatively, read *The Bravest Knight* by Mercer Mayer, a story with little text. Use the knowledge the children gain to collectively create a word web naming all the clothes and armor that a knight might wear. Some children will probably go on to draw and label their own knight at the Drawing/Writing centre during the Literacy and the Arts activity period.

Point out different shields carried by the knights in the texts and in Internet images of knights you find. Talk to the children about the significance of the symbols on a shield, and encourage them to create personal shields to represent themselves and their families. At the Visual Arts centre, the children might draw or paint their chosen crest on cardboard or use materials such as construction paper, string, foil, and paper-towel and toilet-paper rolls.

Consider sharing Shelley Moore Thomas's knight stories too. Thomas wrote a good series of simple, easy-to-read texts. Her titles include *Good Night, Good Knight; Take Care, Good Knight;* and *Happy Birthday, Good Knight*.

Creating an Environment for Success in the Construction Centre

The following section is presented in terms of questions that the reflective practitioner is encouraged to ask about the classroom's Construction centre. The answers reflect what we have found to be best practices.

1. What is my role as teacher at the Construction centre?

- Plan so that the essential learning conditions, as established by Brian Cambourne, are present. As the Introduction: Beyond Worksheets to Learning Centres outlines, these conditions are immersion, demonstration, responsibility, expectation, practice, approximation, and response. Establishing the conditions involves reading texts that are related to building, planning associated Shared Reading and Writing activities, and giving children the right to choose what they are building. It means expecting and encouraging the children to draw pictures of their work or to add signs and captions. It also means readily accepting different levels of response. Schedule time to circulate throughout the room during the Math, Science, and Technology period; you can then offer encouragement, ask questions, listen to explanations, and model various skills and kinds of knowledge.
- Schedule time to visit the children's Construction centre on a regular basis so that you can observe, make suggestions, and track the children's progress.
- Use appropriate vocabulary to extend the children's mathematical, scientific, and technological language: "I noticed that your castle has two turrets that are exactly the same. That's called *symmetry*."
- Ensure that the materials are used in a safe and appropriate manner.

- Collect samples of children's work through photographs and written recordings.
- Provide materials for the children to record the results of their work, perhaps a "Structures Booklet," clipboard and paper, or graph paper.
- Introduce new materials to extend learning or teach new concepts.
- Offer specific challenges to allow children to restate their learning, make connections with other learning, reflect on what they have learned, and pose new questions: "Please explain to me how you were able to make such a tall tower."
- Offer relevant and appropriate mini-lessons to students who need support. For example, you might demonstrate how to use larger blocks at the base of a tower to make it stable or show the children how to use Plexiglas as a platform on which to build.
- Communicate regularly with parents to explain the learning that occurs with construction materials.
- Let the children share and celebrate their efforts and discoveries. Take the children on a walkabout so they can view each other's work with construction materials, water, and sand.

2. How do I ensure that the children and their parents/caregivers see that working at the Construction centre is valuable?

- Schedule time for parents to observe you as the teacher interacting with children at the centre. Once parents see this demonstration and meet to share their observations, they become enthusiastic advocates.
- Record observations of children as they build. Schedule a manageable number of no more than five to observe each day. Be prepared to share your observations of growth with the parents.
- Keep the centre alive, challenging, and well maintained by adding new materials, such as string, cardboard, tinfoil, sticks, pulleys, and props such as people and cars. Children will respond well to its energy.
- Include photographs and simple recordings of the children's work in their portfolios.
- Write a letter to the parents outlining the learning that occurs when children construct.
- Organize a night to share with parents the purpose for the centre and the range of learning that occurs (e.g., from simple stacking to complex balancing or patterning). Create a classroom display for the parents, including both photographs of children's constructions and 3-D displays of blocks set up by the children. Invite parents to build constructions and discuss them to show the learning possibilities.

3. How do I ensure that the materials are easily accessible?

- Provide a number of spaces where these materials can be used — for example, on tables, on the floor, on Plexiglas supported between two blocks — so that the children can view and talk about their structures from many angles.
- Provide opportunities for children to construct independently or with others.
- Provide an appropriate amount of space — big blocks require more space than other materials.
- Determine how this centre will be used in relation to other centres and locate it accordingly, perhaps near the Home/Dramatic Play centre for additional space and materials, or the Visual Arts centre for materials to create props.

(Children are free to use the materials at closed centres to further their play as long as they return the borrowed materials after use.)

- Determine the number of children who can safely and productively work at the centre. Typically, three or four will play with big blocks while about 10 build on available tables or Plexiglas sheets in the room.

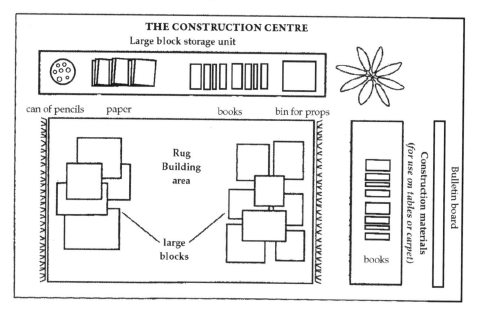

Mileposts to Help Guide Teacher Observations of Children Working at the Construction Centre

When making observations, be sure to remember the developmental nature of children's learning. Skills, knowledge, and interests are not acquired in a lock-step, linear, sequential manner. Children move back and forth on the continuum according to their experiences, circumstances, and materials. The mileposts outlined below are offered merely as a guide — they are not intended to be prescriptive or rigid. It is not expected that all children will demonstrate all of these learnings in the order they are presented. Teachers who listen to and watch their students closely will undoubtedly observe other behavior and learning.

How children show interest in constructing

Children show interest by choosing to build at the Construction centre. They begin to show confidence when building, saying, for example, "I can make a garage like my Dad's." They might take risks, perhaps trying new materials. They build for increasingly long periods of time. They volunteer to share their work and respond when asked about it. They might share their expertise by helping other classmates. They record their work willingly.

How children work at the Construction centre

Children might work in any of the following ways:

- randomly moving the materials from one area to another
- stacking materials and knocking them down
- purposely making towers, using a few materials

- connecting towers and other structures
- using the materials to make an enclosure
- making recognizable structures

The language of number and numeracy that children use

Literacy skills are inextricably linked to the development of concepts and skills found in mathematics, science, and technology activities and in all other areas of the curriculum.

At the Construction centre, children might do any of the following and talk about or record it:

- sorting the materials into groups and explaining the rule used (For example: "I put all the red ones here and all the green ones over here because that way they are not all together and mixed up.")
- ordering the materials and describing the differences in sizes (For example: "This is the biggest and this is the smallest.")
- counting the materials, pointing to each block, and counting accurately (For example: "I counted the number of floors in the building I made, and there are five.")
- counting small groups of materials they have used with one-to-one correspondence (For example: "I have 1, 2, 3, 4, 5, 6, 7, 8 red blocks.")
- classifying materials according to color, shape, and object and then explaining the rule used (For example: "I'll put all the yellow teddy bears in this room; you put all the blues in another room.")
- estimating and checking their guesses of the number of materials used (For example: "I thought I used 100 pieces but when I took my tower down, I counted and found I used only 29.")
- recognizing sets of numbers to 10 (For example: "There are five colored circles on top of each tower.")
- counting by 2s, 5s, and 10s (For example: "When I took my tower down, I counted the pieces by 2s.")
- understanding the concepts of more than, less than, and same as (For example: "Sandra has seven green Duplo and I have four. Sandra has more than I do.")
- recognizing one more than or one fewer than a number of objects (For example: "My tower has one more piece than yours.")
- recording their work in pictorial form and adding captions or a more expanded written form (For example: A child creates a diagram by labelling a drawing of a building with words such as *door*, *roof*, *elevator*, and *basement*.)
- exploring the concepts of addition and subtraction (For example: "Here are five corks. If I take away two, I have three left.")
- exploring the concept of simple fractions (For example: "You can have half the Lego pieces and I'll have the other half.")

The language of geometry that children use

At the Construction centre, children might do any of the following:

- recognizing, naming, and building shapes
- using simple vocabulary to describe their structures (e.g., *behind, beside, on top of*)
- classifying or sorting materials according to shape and explaining the rule used (For example: "I put all the blocks with the same shape together. . . . All

these shapes have four sides. These are rectangles, and these are squares —
each side is the same.")

- identifying geometric shapes in their structures and environment (e.g., recognizing a house as a square)
- accurately naming the geometric shapes, perhaps with other materials, with a picture, or with print
- recognizing symmetry and talking about things that are symmetrical (For example: "The body of a butterfly is the same on both sides.")

The language of data management and probability that children use

At the Construction centre, children might do any of the following:

- collecting or sorting materials
- returning the props to the appropriate container (e.g., putting all the pigs back in the animal container)
- using vocabulary to describe how they have organized the materials (For example: "I put all the blocks here because they are made of wood and all the tubs here because they are made of plastic.")
- recording information using pictures, numbers, shapes, words, tallies, and simple graphs
- predicting what will happen to their structure (For example: "If you take any off this side, it will fall.")
- constructing according to an idea (For example: "I'm going to make a farm with lots of fields for different animals.")
- constructing according to a preconceived plan, perhaps drawn or written

The language of measurement that children use

At the Construction centre, children might do any of the following:

- exploring the concept of measurement (e.g., long, short)
- using measurement vocabulary (e.g., *light, heavy*)
- comparing measurements (e.g., full, empty)
- ordering the materials according to measurement (e.g., small to big)
- using non-standard materials to measure (e.g., toothpicks, hands, feet, blocks of the same size)
- estimating (For example, a child says, "My tower is four hands tall.")
- exploring perimeter (e.g., describes differences and other enclosures)
- exploring volume (e.g., fills containers with buttons or beans) and explaining it
- exploring area (e.g., covers a large block with small blocks) and explaining it
- exploring and explaining mass (For example, a child says, "The big blocks are heavier than the small blocks.")

The language of patterning that children demonstrate

When they use construction materials, children might use the language of patterning:

- identifying a pattern, such as stripes or dots, as well as no pattern (For example: "My building goes like this — red, green, blue, red, green, blue — just like in my shirt.")
- recognizing simple patterns in the environment (For example: "The floor tiles in our room are all squares and they are red and white.")

- pointing out patterns such as color and shape in their structures (For example: "See! I used a yellow and then a red, and it keeps on going like that.")
- creating their own patterns using the materials (For example: "I used three red blocks and then one blue block for my highway.")
- using vocabulary to describe patterns (For example: "My pattern is tricky because it has three different shapes.")
- copying patterns and explaining what they did (For example: "I made my pattern look like your pattern. It has one big block and then a small block. I did it four times like the pattern on the card.")
- extending patterns and explaining their thinking (For example: "I made my pattern longer than yours. I just kept on going and made it look the same every time.")
- recording the patterns they have made using different attributes (e.g., shape, color, size, direction, and number)

The language of science and technology that children use

At the Construction centre, the teacher might observe children doing the following:

- making observations (For example: "It's hard to build a bridge. Mine keeps falling down.")
- asking questions (For example: "Why does it keep falling down?")
- identifying problems (For example: "I think there aren't enough blocks on the sides to hold it up.")
- making predictions about possible outcomes and solutions (For example: "Maybe if I put more blocks on the sides or a longer bit underneath, it will stay up.")
- using simple tools and materials to test hypotheses (For example: "Maybe I'll try a board from the big blocks or a piece of cardboard.")
- describing their observations and making interpretations in order to generalize (For example: "The cardboard didn't work — it's too soft and the board's too heavy. The blocks all fell down again! I think I need a smaller, skinnier board.")
- drawing conclusions (For example: "If the bridge part is too heavy in the middle, then the whole thing will fall down.")

All children love to build and tell others about what they have created. Teachers can capitalize on this natural enthusiasm for construction by introducing literacy concepts and skills. The Construction centre is a dynamic centre. With so many interesting materials and extensions, it can foster and promote oral language development, as well as other literacy skills, such as listening, reading, writing, viewing, and representing.

Reflections for the Journey

All teachers of young children strive to create a positive, learning experience, and with this resource, we have shared the basis for our success in providing this kind of experience. With our collective years of experience and reflection on our practice, we have drawn on our professional journeys to describe a Kindergarten program capable of fostering literacy development. This program capitalized on the interests and motivations of children, and did so without an emphasis on worksheets or a reliance on teacher-directed paper-and-pencil tasks.

We have shared many successful strategies that can support other teachers as they seek to inspire their students and provide programming that meets the children's wide range of developmental levels and interests. These strategies will aid teachers as they help children begin their journeys towards lifelong literacy acquisition. We have also provided teachers with answers to often-asked questions, mileposts to inform teaching instruction, games, specific book titles, and a wealth of literacy extensions that work well at permanent learning centres in the Kindergarten classroom. All of these aids tie in well with the current growing emphasis on the acquisition of literacy.

As noted in the Introduction, Brian Cambourne's conditions of learning provided us with a viable framework for literacy development. These conditions respect basic, traditional tenets of Kindergarten programming, such as learning through play, learning by doing, fostering individual differences, and respecting developmental stages. As is consistent with Cambourne's conditions, we capitalized on the interests of the children. Doing so enabled us to create dynamic permanent centres that provided children with real and authentic reasons to listen, speak, read, write, and view.

Into the centres we infused a wide range of experiences that introduced, motivated, reinforced, and celebrated literacy learning. These experiences included exposure to quality literature and non-fiction, photographs, authentic artifacts, and recording materials. Our play-centred approach was supported by both large- and small-group gatherings and individual activities.

Our Kindergarten programs came to exemplify Cambourne's conditions of learning. Daily, children were *immersed* in an environment that valued and supported literacy through specific activities at each of the centres and at personal reading and writing times. Children were exposed to many *demonstrations* such as models of oral and written language conventions, direct instruction, and positive response during individual and Shared Reading and Writing sessions. We accepted and celebrated *approximations* and recognized that differentiated learning honors individual efforts and abilities. *Expecting* that children would meet with a level of success, we used their attempts and approximations to help us assess and plan for future instruction and activities. A range of quality literature, Buddy Reading, Borrow-a-Book, writing folders, the recording of ideas, and vocabulary-enhancing games all provided real reasons to use and *practise* oral and written language. Individual and small-group gatherings, conferences, and personal interactions throughout the activity periods offered us many opportunities to *celebrate* children's efforts and provide positive *feedback*. We found that the children were truly engaged in their learning because they had the opportunity to share the responsibility for it with the teacher. Able to pursue their own interests and investigations, they understood and accepted ownership of the learning. We were excited that Cambourne's conditions for learning could be so naturally integrated into our Kindergarten programs.

With the infusion of so many literacy experiences into every facet of our program, we could readily demonstrate to children, parents, teachers, and administrators that we had no need to resort to worksheets in order to develop literacy skills. Rather, we proved that by letting children follow their interests and engage in a wide range of activities in a play-based, literacy-rich place, Kindergarten students could meet with literacy success. From their individual levels, they can progress and develop along the continuum of language development, well set on their journey to literacy.

Appendix A: Ways to Record Ideas

This section provides a variety of ideas involving paper, SMART Boards, and hula hoops.

Word Web

A word web is an effective technique to record brainstorming ideas. In the centre of chart paper or on a SMART Board, place the main word, for example, *dinosaurs*, *machines*, or *pets*. As the children offer suggestions, print the word and draw a line to the central word. Continue until all suggestions are recorded. Display this word web at the appropriate centre for the children to use as a reference. Be sure to add pictures to help the children read the print. Below is an example.

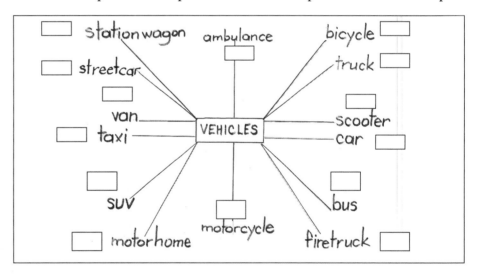

T-Chart

A T-chart is a simple way to record the results of an investigation, such as determining whether materials float or not. Take a large sheet of chart paper or use a SMART Board and draw a line down the middle of the paper or board. Print the two options at the top of the chart, and have the children place the results of their investigations in the correct column. These results can be recorded using either pictures or words.

Things That Float	Things That Do Not Float
boat	marble

Tally

Children can quickly record a total, for example, the number of cups of water it took to fill the water table. Take a strip of paper and fold it, accordion style, into a number of squares. At a Shared Writing session with the large group or with a small group, show how to put a mark in each square for each block used or each cup filled. You might also show the children how to make groups of five for counting larger numbers of objects, for example, ~~IIII~~ 1111.

Cups of Water									Total
/	/	/	/	/	/	/	/	/	9

Venn Diagram

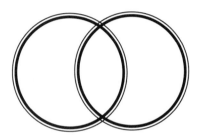

This recording device is useful to help children classify. Take two hula hoops and lay them on the floor, overlapping in the middle so there are three sections. In each section, place a sign or picture to identify which objects can be placed in each section. Use color, plastic models, or shapes. One section might be for animals that live on the land while the other might be for animals that live in the water (see page 114). The overlapping section would display images of animals that live in both the water and on the land. Encourage the children to use pictures, words, or symbols to record the results of their investigations.

Story, or Sequencing, Map

Take a piece of manila or fingerpaint paper. Cut the paper in half and then fold the paper into the desired number of sections. Prompt the children to fill in the different parts of the story. Have them fill in the far left square with the title and the second square with a picture of the beginning of the story; then, guide them to go to the end of the story and fill in the last square. Invite them to select three or four main ideas in the story for the remaining squares. Let them add words to their "pictorial" story map, if they want to. This recording idea should always be modelled at a small-group Shared Writing session with a template prominently displayed for the children to reference. (See page 115 for a child sample.)

Story Map Outline: The 3 Little Pigs

Title	Beginning				Ending
The 3 Little Pigs	Picture of mother pig sending off three little pigs	Picture of first pig's straw house and wolf blowing it down	Picture of second pig's stick house and wolf blowing it down	Picture of third pig's brick house and wolf can't blow it down	Picture of wolf in cauldron in fireplace in the brick house

Voting Sheet

This recording sheet is good for children to vote on their favorite cereal, color, or book. Divide the sheet into the required number of columns. At the top of each column, attach the front of a cereal box, a paint chip, or the cover of a book. During the work period, have each child print his or her name under the option chosen. At the group time, count the votes to make a tally and discuss the results — most, least, more than, and so on.

What is your favorite book?

Spot	Maisy	Corduroy
JOEY	MEI	AnDRE
Fatima	Yu,E	
	MarC	OMAR

In this class vote, children have indicated their preference for books about a particular character.

Human Graph

A human graph is also a good way for children to concretely see data, for example, to compare the number of members in each of the children's families. Make large cards with the numerals 1 to 6. Add a card that says "more than 6." Have the children stand behind the numeral that reflects the number of members in their families. Ask the children in each line to count the number of children composing the line and report to the group. Together, determine which line had the most people and record this information on paper or SMART Board for all to see and discuss.

Shopping List

To encourage the children to make lists, create a blank shopping list for use in the Home/Dramatic Play centre when someone is going to the store. Make several copies of this template. Staple the sheets together to make a small pad. A tip: Ten sheets of 8 1/2 by 11 inch white paper cut vertically in half is a good size. You might add a few pictures of staple items, such as milk and bread, that the children can simply check off.

My Shopping List

crAKrS

MuShRooms

E66S

SoS6IS

ORINGS

A child at the Home centre indicates her intention to buy crackers, mushrooms, eggs, sausages, and oranges.

Sales Receipt

Refer to the outline below to make a small receipt booklet for the children to use when giving receipts for materials purchased — for example, for goods (shoes, food, airline ticket) or for services rendered (a new hairstyle or teeth cleaning). These receipts can be used with a number of the literacy extensions associated with the Home/Dramatic Play centre, for example, shoe store, grocery store, travel agency, hair salon, or dentist's office.

Store Receipt

Store Name No FRiLLS

Server DAVID

Date SuNDAy JAN. 12 2011

Item Bought APPLES (20)

Cost 3.99 30% OFF

A child at a grocery store extension of the Home/Dramatic Play centre has printed out a receipt.

Order Pads

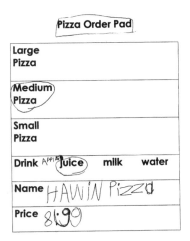

Pizza Order Pad

Large Pizza	
Medium Pizza	
Small Pizza	
Drink APPle Juice   milk   water
Name HAWiN Pizza
Price 8.90

Make a number of small order pads for the children to use when taking an order in a restaurant or over the phone for a pizza delivery. Consider putting in some information to make the process easier for the beginning writers, for example, a combination of pictures and words, maybe different sizes of wedges for different sizes of pizza. This recording technique needs to be developed with a small group of children in a Shared Writing session. One child-completed template we have used is shown.

Other templates we have used include simple cheque outlines and address books. Templates are always most effective if created with the children who want to use them for a literacy extension.

Appendix B: Games

Concentration

Each of the following games can be stored in a Ziploc bag for the children to use throughout the activity period. Encourage the children to record their results on a scorecard and include blank recording sheets for the children to use with the game. Later, the children can glue the results into Games booklets. Stickers and Internet clip art are very useful tools in making the following games.

Concentration can relate to any centre in the classroom depending on the children's interest and the current extensions for their literacy learning. For example, the game could include food images from the Home/Dramatic Play centre, underwater creatures from the aquarium at the Water centre, or bakery items from the bakery at the Sand centre.

Concentration helps children develop their visual memory, visual discrimination skills, conversation, use of new vocabulary, and co-operative play skills. It is a good game for two children to play.

MATERIALS

20 blank playing cards or pieces of cardboard (to yield 10 matching pairs) stickers or markers for drawing images

NOTES:

1. Depending on the children's developmental levels, there are several ways to make this game and adjust the level of difficulty. Pairs could be
   - two matching images (e.g., two pictures of a turtle)
   - an image and the matching initial consonant (e.g., a picture of a turtle and the letter *t*)
   - an image and the corresponding word (e.g., a picture of a turtle and the word *turtle*)
2. As the children become more proficient players, the teacher may want to add more pairs to increase the level of difficulty.

INSTRUCTIONS

The player with the most pairs wins.

1. Lay all the cards on the table face down.
2. One at a time, each child turns over two cards looking for a match.
3. If a match has not been made, the cards must be put back in the same place and then the next player takes a turn.
4. If a match has been made, the player gets another turn.

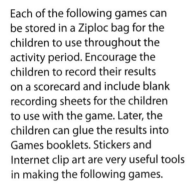

This is a hand-made laminated card, one of a set for matching baby animals.

It is important for the children to record their results. This recording can be done in the Drawing/Writing Book. Some children might draw a picture of themselves playing with another child, some children might print a short label saying, "I won!" and other children might print a full sentence about how many pairs they were able to collect. For a child not yet able to represent with pictures and words, the teacher might take a photograph of the child playing the game.

Bingo

This game helps children develop their visual memory, auditory discrimination skills and, depending on the materials used, sound–symbol relationships, as well as knowledge and memory of key sight vocabulary. It also familiarizes the children with the letters of the alphabet and matching pictures with initial consonants.

MATERIALS (based on four players)

boards with 3, 4, or 5 spaces across and a corresponding number of spaces down (one board per player)
blank cards — 36, 64, or 100, depending on board size
stickers, words, or pictures
tokens for each player — 9, 16, or 25, depending on board size

NOTES:

Notes and instructions apply to nine-square boards.

1. Each player needs a board that shows eight pictures or words that are reflective of the selected literacy extension; the board should also show a "free space." Some boards must contain the same pictures or words. Boards can be prepared in several ways: the children can draw pictures or cut them out of magazines and paste them onto the boards, or you can provide stickers to be used on the boards. Print the name of the object under each picture.
2. This game can be expanded to include initial consonants. On each of 32 of the cards, put a picture, sticker, or word that is identical to something found on the boards. Remember to repeat some of the pictures, stickers, or words so the players have many chances to cover a Bingo square.

INSTRUCTIONS

The first player to cover all squares wins.

1. Each player takes a board.
2. The pack of 36 calling cards is placed face down on the table.
3. Each player in turn takes a card.
4. If a player has a match, he or she covers the appropriate square with a token.

For Food Bingo, for example, a laminated Bingo card might show stickers and handwritten words for banana, cookie, hamburger, watermelon, carrot, ice cream, strawberry, and pizza, as well as a square marked "a free space." A card size of 23 cm by 30.5 cm (9 by 12 inches), with each square 7.5 cm by 7.5 cm (3 inches) works well.

Track Games

This game helps children practise counting with one-to-one correspondence, and depending upon the Chance cards, it promotes understanding of sound–letter relationships, oral comprehension, and recognition of key words from one of the centres. It also helps children practise left-to-right progression.

MATERIALS

track board made out of a sheet of bristol board (Make the board in sections so it can be taped together for use but folded up for storage.)
dice or spinner
different markers, one per player

3 to 4 Chance cards depending on the level of development of the children playing (The teacher can add more Chance cards as the children become more proficient players.)

NOTES:

1. Track games can be adapted to help children practise a variety of skills. We suggest making generic track boards that can be adapted by changing game components. Make the track with squares or shapes on it and with a box for Start and a box for Finish. At strategic places along the route, place hazard squares (e.g., Go back 3 spaces) and bonus squares (e.g., Go forward 2 spaces).
2. The reading component comes in using the Chance cards. If a player lands on a Chance square, he or she must take a card from the pile and read or identify the picture. Suggestions for what to put on the Chance cards include these:
   * letters of the alphabet (The player must say a word that starts with the letter sound before going on.)
   * instructions to point out something (For example: Find something that begins with *B*.)
   * words from the selected centre (e.g., *shark*, *porpoise*, and *whale* for a game at the aquarium extension at the Water centre)

INSTRUCTIONS

The first player to reach the end wins.

1. Place the board in the centre of the table or on the floor.
2. Each player selects a marker.
3. All players place a marker at the start.
4. Players take turns rolling the dice (or using the spinner) and moving their marker the appropriate number of spaces.
5. If a player lands on a Chance square, he or she must correctly answer the question. Players who can't answer correctly miss a turn.

Playing with Collections

Children love to play with collections, sorting them, lining them up, and making up stories and games. Mix two collections and ask the children to sort them. Include a set of labels and have the children match the words to the appropriate objects (e.g., things from the sea, objects whose names start like Mary's name). Children can also play I Spy in pairs, using only objects. These activities help children begin to identify sounds of the alphabet and to match the sounds to the appropriate letters. They also help children to sort and classify objects. Collections provide children with the opportunity to share orally or in pictures the rule they used for sorting.

Hannah's Collections by Marthe Jocelyn is a heart-warming story of a child who collects many things and sorts them by size, shape, and color.

Encourage the children to collect objects that represent the letters of the alphabet or that you can use for different literacy extensions. Children can help by bringing objects from home (e.g., plastic dinosaurs, shells, and stamps). At garage sales, you can likely find unique materials at a limited cost. You might fill an old suitcase with items whose names, for example, all start with the same letter (a toy cat, a car, a doll's coat, a card, a candy). If possible, find tiny things that can be placed in a shoebox.

Jaws

Jaws is a fast-paced version of a track game played between two people. Depending on the question cards, it helps children identify pictures or read significant words (nouns) by sight. Jaws also helps children to practise one-to-one counting skills. Children find it fun to play.

MATERIALS

cardboard strip at least 10 cm (4 inches) long and 12.5 cm (5 inches) deep
small pieces of cardboard
question cards with pictures, words, or simple questions
plastic bags
images of two creatures, where one is the enemy of the other

NOTES:

1. Make a track by folding a strip of cardboard into zigzags (accordion style) — the folds represent waves or obstacles. Each player makes a cardboard figure or selects a sticker where one image is the enemy of the other image (e.g., a plant-eating dinosaur and a meat-eating dinosaur).
2. Design the question cards to support any of the literacy extensions. For example, at the Dinosaur Land in the Sand centre, the cards can have different pictures or names of dinosaurs that the players must identify or read.
3. Keep game variations in plastic bags, for example, a pig and a wolf, or a swimmer and a shark.

INSTRUCTIONS

1. Players place the figures at the left end of the strip.
2. At each turn a player must pick up a question card and read the word or identify the picture.
3. A correct identification permits the player to move one wave or mountain (depending on the setting); a wrong answer means the player stays in the same place.
4. If the victim (e.g., plant eater) gets to the end of the cardboard strip first, it wins. If the enemy (e.g., meat eater) gets there first, the victim is in trouble and loses.

Go Fish

This game helps encourage young children who need practice in asking questions. Initially, it will be necessary to help the children ask each other questions, for example, "Do you have a dump truck?" "Do you have a bus?"

MATERIALS

two sets of blank playing cards with the same picture on each pair (e.g., bulldozer, dump truck, bus, train); at least 10 pairs of pictures in total

INSTRUCTIONS

The player with the most pairs wins the game.

1. Each player picks up four cards from the deck placed in the middle of the playing surface.
2. The first player asks, "Do you have a . . . ?"
3. If the other player has that picture, then he or she gives it up.
4. When a player has a match, the cards are set aside, and the player gets another turn.
5. If the opponent cannot provide a match, then the player picks up from the deck. If he or she picks up a match, the cards are then set aside.
6. Players take turns until all the cards are played.

Snap

This game helps children develop their oral language and attention span. It can be created to support any of the literacy extensions (e.g., Shoe Snap, Zoo Snap, or Dinosaur Snap). The game could also be created for a specific literacy skill, for example, Alphabet Snap, where half the letters are capital letters and the other half are lower case letters. Snap is a good game for two children to play.

MATERIALS

a deck of 52 cards created, with two of each sticker or letter of the alphabet

INSTRUCTIONS

The player who ends up with all the cards in the deck wins.

1. Divide the deck into two even piles, one for each player.
2. Players in turn place a card from their pile face up on the playing surface.
3. When a match is made, the player who notices and calls "Snap" first takes the pile.

Tic Tac Toe

This game helps young children to identify pictures, letters, and sight words, as well as to problem-solve and see patterns.

MATERIALS

one board ruled into nine squares, three across and three down; on each square put a picture (perhaps a sticker), letter, or significant word (e.g., names of the children in the class or words from a literacy extension).
two sets of markers (e.g., poker chips, small stones)

NOTE:

It is helpful to make several of these boards using different pictures and words.

INSTRUCTIONS

The first player to cover three squares in a row wins.

1. The first player covers a square with a marker. To stay on that square the player must identify the picture or letter or read the word.
2. The next player repeats the process and tries to prevent three squares in a row from being covered.

Appendix C: Recipes for Visual Arts Activities

See Chapter 5: The Visual Arts Centre.

Cooked Playdough

Ingredients

1½ cups / 375 ml salt
2 cups / 500 ml flour
4 teaspoons cream of tartar
2 tablespoons cooking oil
2 cups / 500 ml water
food coloring

Each week, parents can help to make fresh playdough for the Kindergarten at home. One family per week can make a different color. A class parent can coordinate the assignment dates. As the children become more familiar with the material, a small group can make it during an activity time, with the supervision of a parent volunteer.

METHOD

Mix all ingredients in a saucepan.
Add food coloring.
Cook on medium heat for 3 to 5 minutes.*
Stir constantly until the mixture becomes stiff.
Cool and store in airtight containers.
* An adult should do this.

Flour-and-Salt Modelling Material

Ingredients

1 tablespoon cooking oil
1 cup / 250 ml water
food coloring
2 cups / 500 ml flour
1 cup / 250 ml salt

Parents can be most helpful in making fresh flour-and-salt modelling material for the classroom.

METHOD

Mix food coloring with oil and water.
Add to the dry ingredients.
If the dough becomes sticky, add some flour.
Store in plastic containers or bags.

Clay

Ingredients

1 cup / 250 ml cornstarch
2 cups / 500 ml baking soda
1½ cups / 375 ml cold water

Clay is a good medium for children to use when making three-dimensional models, perhaps of people or animals. It seems to work well for models that have to stand. Unlike other modelling materials, clay can be painted.

METHOD

Mix cornstarch and baking soda together.
Add water.
Cook over a medium heat.

Stir constantly until the mixture looks like moist, mashed potatoes.
Pour mixture on a plate and cover with a damp cloth.
When mixture cools, knead it like dough.
To prevent sticking, work on wax paper or dust the utensils with cornstarch.
Use only a little clay at a time, storing the rest in an airtight container.

String Painting

Ingredients

thickened poster paint
string of different thicknesses
several pie plates to hold paint
manila or construction paper

This technique motivates much conversation, prediction, and speculation.

METHOD

Provide aprons or old shirts to cover up clothes.
Work on a table or the floor covered with an oilcloth or newspapers.
Place a piece of string in one of the plates of paint.
Drag the covered string over the paper.
Return the string to the appropriate color.
Repeat with different thicknesses of string and colors.

Fingerpainting

Ingredients

powder paint and starch or
commercial fingerpaint
fingerpaint paper

As well as providing a creative learning experience and oral language development, this technique can be used to provide an excellent background for other works of art.

METHOD

Work on an oilcloth on the floor or a table covered with newsprint.
Place paint in a number of beakers.
Pour some paint on the fingerpaint paper.
Show the children how to use their hands to make a design or pattern. Discuss parts of the hand and share ideas for making different designs.
Direct the children to add different colors if they wish.
Provide a bucket with warm water and soap for washing hands, as well as aprons or old shirts to cover clothes.
Provide sponges for cleanup.
Be sure to let children show their efforts at a celebration or Gathering Time.

Marbles in a Box

Ingredients

marbles
different-colored paint
small boxes
construction or manila paper

This technique is excellent for making backgrounds for collage projects or covers for children's class-made books.

METHOD

Line the bottom of a small box with construction paper.
Squirt a few dabs of different-colored paint on the paper.
Add several marbles to the box.
Gently roll the marbles around to make a pattern.
Carefully remove the paper and dry.

Sponge and Print Making

Ingredients

sponges
"found" materials (print makers)
mural, manila, or painting paper (18 by 24 inches)
paints of different colors in disposable tinfoil pie plates

This painting technique is good for creating a quick background for murals and other large pieces of work.

METHOD

Provide plastic aprons or old workshirts to cover up clothes.
Work on a table covered with oilcloth or newspapers.
Place different-colored paint in individual tinfoil pie plates.
Provide a selection of small sponges or found materials (e.g., buttons, spools).
Demonstrate different ways to dip the print maker into the paint.
Remind the children to use different print makers for each color of paint.
Provide sponges and a bucket of water to clean up the work area.

Papier Mâché

Ingredients

newspapers torn into half-sheet size
masking tape
commercial wallpaper paste, if available, or thinned white glue

This activity is good to use to make 3-D round pieces of fruit such as apples, oranges, or pumpkins.

METHOD

Demonstrate to the children how to crush one piece of newspaper together.
Have the children work with a partner and tape the crushed ball of newsprint into a ball. Use lots of tape to secure this beginning ball of paper.
Add layers of newspaper until the ball is the necessary size.
Make other balls or rolls of paper to serve as arms, legs, and so on.
Tape the additional balls or rolls of paper to the initial ball of newspaper shapes.
Demonstrate how to place a large piece of tissue paper on the newspaper form and cover with white glue.
Continue the process until the whole structure is covered with tissue paper.
Leave to dry overnight.
Repeat the gluing process over several days.

Crushed Tissue

Ingredients

2 inch by 2 inch (5 cm by 5 cm) different-colored tissue paper, circular or square in shape, in tinfoil pie plates or small boxes
thinned white glue in plastic containers (e.g., small yogurt containers)
glue brushes
mural, or manila, paper for the outline of the creature
markers

This art activity is good for covering the body of a large creature such as a fish, shark, or dinosaur. Display space and the children's ideas will determine the animal's size.

METHOD

Work on an oilcloth or a large, washable table.
Have the children draw the outline of their creature on mural paper.
Show the children how to twist a piece of tissue paper on the end of a finger or pencil to make the tissue stand up or how to "scrunch" or "crush" each tissue piece into a ball.
Dip the end of the ball into the thinned glue.
Press the crushed tissue on the surface to be covered.
Show the children how to place each tissue close together, filling in all the spaces within the outline.

Index